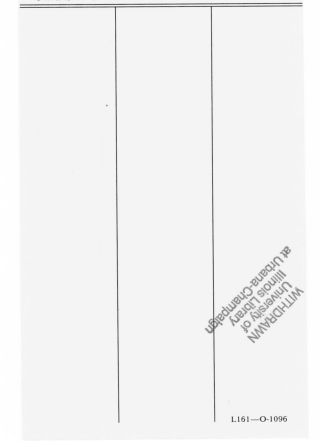

THE HERMITAGE MUSEUM
LENINGRAD

FRENCH PAINTING

SECOND HALF OF THE 19th TO EARLY 20th CENTURY

THE HERMITAGE MUSEUM
L E N I N G R A D

A COMPLETE PUBLICATION
OF THE COLLECTION
WITH 358 COLOUR PLATES,
INCLUDING 44 DETAILS

AURORA ART PUBLISHERS. LENINGRAD

COMPILED BY ANNA BARSKAYA
INTRODUCED BY ANTONINA IZERGHINA
NOTES ON THE PLATES BY ANNA BARSKAYA
DESIGNED BY VLADIMIR SMOLKOV
TRANSLATED BY PHILIPPA HENTGÈS (INTRODUCTION)
AND YURI PAMFILOV

Ф $\frac{80103\text{-}436}{023(01)\text{-}76}$ 56-76

THE PRESENT EDITION is devoted to the Hermitage collection of modern French painting, starting from the Pre-Impressionist period and ending with the artistic trends which originated before World War I. These canvases come chiefly from the big and already well-known collections that had belonged to two Moscow connoisseurs, Ivan Abramovich Morozov and Sergei Ivanovich Shchukin. The work of these two men cannot be overestimated, and indeed, had long attracted the attention of experts. It is remarkable that in those years, when the reputation of the new French painting was still to be made in France itself, there appeared so far away in Moscow some of the finest canvases by the French artists of the time who were to become the classical masters of European painting at the end of the nineteenth century and the beginning of the twentieth. How can we explain the fact that both in choice and in number these collections were so outstanding as to be the envy of all collectors in France and other countries? The answer is again to be found in the history of the collections, and especially in the events that influenced French art at the time when the collections were being made. They were stormy years, particularly the first fifteen of this century. It was a time of a search for new ideas and new means of expression, which was to mark a new stage in the history of the fine arts. Today, when we look back on history that is more than half-a-century old, the changes that art was undergoing seem clear and understandable, even inevitable from the historical point of view. All that went to influence painting in the early twentieth century is now widely known. In a host of papers, anthologies, and text-books the principal art trends have been defined and the names of their most typical exponents acknowledged. But the immediate witnesses of these events could not evaluate them with such precision. They only saw the apparent confusion in which it was difficult to make a distinction between the essential and the unessential, between the important and the accidental.

Today we can recognize the positive achievements of the early years of the century. But those who lived through this time saw it as an open battle that had become even more bitter than the sallies of the previous century. No one knew who would win the day, for the young artists who represented the new trends came up against a still more stubborn enemy and a still greater lack of understanding than had their predecessors. The only painters who gradually began to win recognition, however cautious it may have been, during the first ten years of the twentieth century were the Impressionists who had been striving for recognition for nearly forty years and who had by that time lost several of their main representatives. Alfred Sisley and Berthe Morisot did not live to see success, and Camille Pissarro could only feel it drawing near when he died in 1903. The victory of the new principles was, however, hardly discernible, for it was hidden beneath an endless number of everyday events that showed the tenacity of outlived conceptions. To give an example of these early successes we may refer to a series of retrospective exhibitions devoted to the works of the finest Post-Impressionists, such as Van Gogh (1901), Toulouse-Lautrec (1902), Seurat (1905), Gauguin (1906) and Cézanne (1907). Despite the great influence they had on the younger generation, these exhibitions did not meet with general appraisal.

The decision to organize an annual Salon d'Automne in 1903, whose jury was made up of the more liberal painters, was a democratic measure that certainly helped to pave the way for the coming generation of artists. It is true that the Salons des Indépendants still continued to function, but it is sufficient to look at their catalogues to see that each one contained only an insignificant number of canvases by artists that determined the history of twentieth century painting. As in the past, in the official Salons of the nineteenth century, these truly talented painters exhibited alongside poor imitators and eclectics who still

5

retained a dominant position. Even in the famous Salon d'Automne of 1905, where the so-called Fauves really did cause a sensation, there were, out of all the sixteen hundred and thirty-six paintings hung, only five by Matisse, three by Manguin, two by Derain and a small number by Vlaminck, Rouault, Jean Puy, Marquet and Friesz. We should not forget that at the height of the Fauvist movement Matisse had to put himself down in the catalogues as "Henri" in order to distinguish his work from that of an Auguste Matisse, who is now quite forgotten. And if the official critics took notice of these young innovators, they did so in order to bring down upon them laughter and scorn, just as cruel and shortsighted as the reproaches that had been thrown at the Impressionists. It is sad to note that even the shrewder critics who showed sympathy for the new trend failed to recognize Matisse, who remains one of the greatest painters of our day. Finally, when in 1907 Picasso finished his fundamental work, *Les Demoiselles d'Avignon*, all the critics forsook him. "Picasso tells us that one day Fénéon [...] came to the rue Ravignan, at Bateau-Lavoir, to see him, and saw *Les Demoiselles d'Avignon*. Fénéon said to Picasso, 'You ought to draw caricatures!' And Fénéon, Picasso adds, was someone." [1]

This, then, was the state of affairs existing in French art during the first years of the century. Roughly speaking, artists were divided into the recognized and the unrecognized. The Russian connoisseurs who went to Paris at that time came up against the confusion and the "polyphonous" character of art that had thrown the nineteenth century collectors off their stride. However, unlike their predecessors, Shchukin and Morozov had a very advanced attitude. They did not hesitate, they did not choose "a little of everything". On the contrary, they followed their instincts in buying pictures by these young artists. They bought the works of artists that had just been recognized, of those who were beginning to win recognition and of some who remained quite unknown. And this was the secret of their unprecedented success.

In a very short time, within some ten or twelve years, two outstanding collections were assembled which included first-class works of the Impressionists and Post-Impressionists: Monet, Pissarro, Renoir, Degas, Cézanne, Van Gogh, Gauguin, Signac, Cross, Henri Rousseau, as well as a large number of Fauvist canvases. Apart from fifty paintings by Matisse, there was also the work of his followers, such as Derain, Marquet, Vlaminck, Friesz, Puy and Manguin. Between them Morozov and Shchukin bought fifty-four Picassos. These two collectors did not merely buy what they saw; for their Moscow homes they ordered great decorative paintings from the artists of the younger generation, including Bonnard, Maurice Denis and Matisse; thanks to them, some fine samples of monumental French painting of the period found their way into Russia. Of course, this avant-garde French painting attracted others besides Russians. Many large collections of the Impressionists were already formed by the end of the century (those of Moreau-Nélaton, Camondo, Faure), while a large number of Matisse's and Picasso's pictures were bought by members of the Stein family. But none of these art-lovers made so many or such widespread purchases as the two Russians. As time went on, especially after World War I, the significance of the French art of this period became increasingly apparent. In Europe and in the United States French paintings of the late nineteenth and early twentieth centuries began to be sought after and bought at exorbitant prices. However, by that time many of the best works had become inaccessible to European and American buyers, being in the possession of Soviet museums.

---

[1] Hélène Parmelin, *Picasso. Les Dames de Mougins*, Paris, 1964, p. 90.

The fact that these collections were amassed in Russia becomes easier to understand if one analyses the history of the period, considering not only the arts in France but also what was happening in Russia. At the turn of the century—when the first Russian revolution of 1905 was imminent—the younger artists were searching for new ways of expression: new forms, new perspectives, new potential. Morozov and Shchukin followed all new trends with great attention. Shchukin associated closely with both artists and critics, while Morozov acquired a large number of paintings by his contemporaries, making his collection of Russian art one of the most interesting of the time. The canvases of Korovin, Vrubel, Konchalovsky, Mashkov and Golovin, and later those of Utkin, Saryan, Chagall and Larionov were hung on the walls of his Moscow house which, like Shchukin's, was fast becoming a private museum. It was their love for contemporary Russian art that guided both Morozov and Shchukin in their interest and understanding of contemporary art in France. They sought to compare the development of art in Russia and in Europe in general, looking for trends that were common to the art of their day as a whole and for the differences that distinguished the French and the Russian schools. This is why Morozov hung the canvases of Konchalovsky and Cézanne together in one room. And because there existed in Russia a marked enthusiasm for all the arts at that time, Morozov and Shchukin were not alone in the work they did. For example, Sergei Shchukin's brother Piotr, who specialized in old Russian art, was also interested in modern French painting. Certainly he did not do much buying, but his collection contained such famous canvases as *Nude* by Renoir, *Lady in the Garden* by Claude Monet, *Woman Combing Her Hair* by Degas, and Maurice Denis' *Sacred Grove*. He obviously felt that these canvases were somewhat out of place in the public museum set up by him (which was even built in the old Russian style), and was more than willing to sell them to his brother Sergei.

An outstanding connoisseur, whose initiative and taste did much to build up the Russian museums, was Ivan Morozov's brother Mikhail, who died in 1903 while still quite young. Apart from his collection of Pre-Impressionist painting, which included Daubigny's landscape *Banks of the Oise*, he bought a big portrait by Renoir of the French actress Jeanne Samary, Edouard Manet's *Cabaret*, Monet's *Poppy Field*, *After the Bath* by Degas, two Gauguin landscapes and a seascape by Van Gogh. Mikhail Morozov's collection was donated to the Tretyakov Gallery by his widow in 1910 and remained in that museum until 1925, completing the Barbizon School collection made by Sergei Tretyakov.

The work done to make French and other foreign art better known to the Russian public was continued by the organization of annual international exhibitions which presented a great number of paintings by Western European and American artists. It is true that the new trends were not very well represented at these exhibitions, but as far back as the winter of 1898—99 the Society for the Encouragement of the Arts in St Petersburg held an exhibition of French painting showing the works of Monet, Pissarro, Sisley, and Renoir. The Russian press regularly published reports of such exhibitions, as well as articles devoted to the new trends in French painting, accompanied by photographs of new works.

The growing interest in French painting and its comparison with Russian art of the period led to the two Moscow exhibitions of 1908 and 1909, organized by the art review *Zolotoye Runo* (*The Golden Fleece*), which included both French and Russian canvases. The 1908 exhibition was one of the biggest shows of French Post-Impressionism ever to have been held before the war. While somewhat unsystematic in character, it was nevertheless of great importance. The latest works of such Russian painters as Saryan, Pavel Kuznetsov, Utkin,

Petrov-Vodkin and Larionov were hung beside those of Matisse, Marquet, Van Gogh, Gauguin, Braque, Vuillard. Looking back now, it is difficult to explain why Shchukin and Morozov paid so little attention to this exhibition. Other connoisseurs bought a certain number of works; N. P. Riabushinsky, editor of *Zolotoye Runo*, bought Van Dongen's *Dancer in Red* and Rouault's *Filles*, Dessek bought Van Dongen's *Woman in Black Gloves*, Ya. N. Liapunov bought Vuillard's *Divan* and S. A. Poliakov, editor of the journal *Vesy (The Scales)*, bought Le Fauconnier's *Lake*.

Thus, it is clear that French art was becoming widely known, and that the interest shown in it by Shchukin and Morozov was by no means exclusive. This can be seen, too, from the fact that in making their purchases the two collectors were guided by several advisors, some of whom were true experts. Artists, critics and writers were pleased to see that the acquisitions of these two Moscow connoisseurs were not only the result of "a passion for collecting", but showed as well that they were ready to put their exceptionally vast fortunes to good use. And this was something that other Russian collectors could not do. Despite the private nature of these two collections, they came to be regarded, rather as the royal collections of the eighteenth century had been, as Russian property which, at some future time, would be turned over to the public. Indeed, the owners themselves fostered this idea, openly saying how they intended to bequeath their property to the city of Moscow: in this they followed in the steps of the many Russian connoisseurs of the preceding century. Even during their lifetime their collections were open to visitors. The work of Shchukin and Morozov took on a public character, which enabled many other outstanding representatives of Russian culture to contribute to it, and here the best painters played an important role. Igor Grabar, who often travelled abroad, frequently told Morozov of works which he thought should be bought in France. When Ivan Morozov, accompanied by Valentin Serov, visited a Druet exhibition in Paris, he also bought two fine Van Goghs, *The Prison Courtyard* and *Red Vineyards at Arles*. Surikov and other leading painters gave much time to building up these collections.

The long-standing connections that both Shchukin and Morozov maintained in Paris were yet another reason why such first-class collections could be assembled in Moscow. They were regular visitors to all the Paris exhibitions, especially those devoted to the younger generation of artists, such as the Salon des Indépendants and the Salon d'Automne, and were often to be found in the artists' studios. They were well known to all the most famous Paris dealers, such as Durand-Ruel, Vollard, Bernheim and, later on, Kahnweiler, who were the best connoisseurs of the new French painting, and regularly sent canvases from their galleries to Moscow. Letters, accounts and invoices signed by these well-known dealers arrived more and more frequently in Moscow's Bolshoi Znamensky Lane and Prechistenka Street (today Kropotkin Street). Letters from painters arrived there, too—from Matisse, Bonnard, Vuillard, Maurice Denis. Letters from the rue Laffitte, where Vollard had his shop, were more often addressed to Morozov's office in Varvarka (now Razin Street), while letters from Kahnweiler of the rue Vignon went to Znamensky Lane where Shchukin lived. For the two Russian collectors tended to keep apart, each developing his particular preferences.

Although Morozov was twenty years younger than Shchukin, his taste was more "classical". At first he concentrated on Russian art and began buying French paintings much later than Shchukin did, taking up this new line because he wished to continue the work of his brother Mikhail who had died in 1903. Morozov gradually acquired an understanding of art and a clearness of purpose, shaping the character of his collection step by step as it expanded. At first he would often buy paintings of little account which he later weeded out as he himself became more demanding. He was attracted by the Impressionists, buying paintings by Monet, Renoir and Sisley. He was particularly fond of Cézanne and in purchasing his paintings showed great singleness of purpose: he made up his mind to acquire a work of Cézanne's later period and for a long time kept a vacant space on his wall until he bought the *Blue Landscape*, a particularly fine example of the artist's late manner.

Morozov also purchased a large number of Gauguin's paintings, most of which belonged to the first Tahiti period when the artist's work did not possess a truly innovatory character. Morozov had liked Bonnard from the start, and all except two of the works of this painter in Soviet museums come from his collection (of these two, one was bought by his brother Mikhail and the other was given to the Hermitage by the Leningrad collector L. Rybakova). Long before the artist was well-known, Morozov invited him to paint five decorative panels for the hall of his Moscow house. Morozov also showed his preference for more traditional forms when he ordered the great decorative panels destined for the reception rooms of his town house from Maurice Denis, who was then seeking to bring back classical traditions in his mural painting. Morozov disliked the work of Henri Rousseau and was indifferent to Cubism; of his three Picasso paintings, only one belongs to the Cubism period. It seems that he did not make the personal acquaintance of Picasso, for on June 5, 1911 Vollard wrote to him: "Monsieur, since I have been in the country for some days, I have only just received your request for information as to the name of Picasso, which is Pablo..."[2] On the other hand, Morozov was enthusiastic about Fauvism and bought Fauve canvases by Derain, Friesz, Manguin and Valtat, as well as many particularly well-chosen paintings by Matisse, to whom he was introduced in 1908 by Shchukin. When he first began to take an interest in Matisse, Morozov picked out his early pictures, but later, perhaps influenced by Shchukin, he acquired a taste for Matisse and bought the best works of the artist's Moroccan period.

Shchukin was of a very different nature. His taste, too, was formed step by step. At the end of the nineties, when he started his collection, he bought a certain number of rather poor works by artists who had responded, but more timidly, to the new artistic ideas. These included such painters as Cottet, Lucien Simon and Lobre, who exhibited in the more official Salon du Champ-de-Mars. The only interesting acquisitions made by Shchukin at the outset of his career as a collector were three works by Redon and a fine study by Puvis de Chavannes for his painting *A Poor Fisherman*. But Shchukin's taste soon began to change when the Russian painter Fiodor Botkin, who had long lived in Paris, drew his attention to the Impressionists. In 1898 Shchukin bought from Durand-Ruel one of the first Monets to be seen in Russia, *Lilac in Argenteuil*, and from that moment on he devoted all his enthusiasm and energy to the new French painting.

It happens that the archive material on these two connoisseurs is very uneven. There are many documents relating to the work of the reserved and jealous Morozov, which give a clear indication of the way he gradually completed his gallery. But there is hardly anything to tell us about the way the lively and sociable Shchukin went about it. We can only see the development of his taste in his collection as it finally came down to us. It contains the best works of the Impressionists—Renoir, Monet and Degas, while the Post-Impressionists are represented by Van Gogh and Cézanne; in choosing the works of the latter, Shchukin went further than Morozov. Cézanne's still lifes in the Morozov collection were received by the

---

[2] See Архив ГМИИ, фонд № 13, опись 1, единица хранения H/11, лист 18 [Archives of the Museum of Modern Western Art, now at the Pushkin Museum of Fine Arts, Moscow].

9

Moscow public more or less calmly, but Shchukin was met by mockery when he bought the figure composition *Carnival*. However, he was not deterred. He next bought two Tahiti landscapes by Gauguin, although he was not certain then that his choice had been correct. In his general attitude towards art, Shchukin was rather peculiar. When he came up against something that was unknown and unusual, he would at first recoil, only to become, shortly afterwards, a passionate admirer of all that had at first repelled him. This was why he used to say that every picture should "hang before his eyes" for some time before he understood it. But as time went on, this period of adaptation became shorter and shorter. Shchukin "became used to Gauguin" very quickly and in a short space of time he had purchased eleven more canvases by him. Later he was caught up by a new wave of enthusiasm and bought a large number of works by Picasso and Matisse. It was characteristic of him that when he first saw Picasso's *Les Demoiselles d'Avignon* he felt disheartened. Referring to Picasso, whose earlier works he had acquired, he cried, "What a loss for French painting!" But very soon afterwards he was buying a whole series of paintings from Picasso's early Cubist period, including a later version of the picture that had so much upset him. Like Morozov, Shchukin was sometimes cautious in his attitude to quite unknown painters. For instance, he only bought one Braque and completely ignored Juan Gris. Kahnweiler, who knew Shchukin well, says that he regarded Picasso as an artist "with a past" who had been through his "Blue" and "Pink" periods, while at that time Braque was less known and Juan Gris, who began as a Cubist, had not yet managed to get himself recommended. It was the same thing with Matisse. Shchukin was most enthusiastic about this painter and had regularly visited his studio from 1908 on, but he was shocked when he saw *The Dance* and *Music*, the panels which Matisse had painted to his order and which, in daring, outshone all that the painter had previously attempted. Shchukin's reaction made Matisse very unhappy, for he had looked upon him as his patron. Soon, however, Shchukin became enamoured of these works and in 1913 he bought the big canvas called *Arab Coffee-house* which, in its simplified lines and uninhibited colour, was typical of Matisse's revolutionary break with conventional means.

In the course of seven or eight years Shchukin had assembled that part of his collection which proved to be quite unique. The high level of the Impressionist and Post-Impressionist painting in the two Russian collections can be found in other museums abroad, but nowhere else can one find such a wealth of Fauve and early Cubist works as Shchukin had assembled. Alfred Barr, one of the foremost authorities on twentieth century art, called the Shchukin collection "the greatest collection in the world, public or private, of French paintings of the early 20th century school of Paris, many of them purchased almost before their paint was dry".[3] The German art critic Otto Grautoff, who visited Moscow in 1919, was also astounded at the richness of the Shchukin collection which he described as "one of the few contemporary galleries which were not created for speculative purposes or in the desire to win praise".[4]

The new spirit evident in this collection was best characterized by Igor Grabar, the painter and critic, in his memoirs, when he said: "Shchukin was, by nature and temperament, a collector of a lively, active art, the art of today or, more correctly, of tomorrow. He was comforted by the thought that the pictures he bought were not to be found in museums, and therefore cost very little. This view was dictated not by niggardliness but by the sporting turn of mind of a man eager to make a mock of the thick-headed rich men who did

---

[3] Alfred Barr, *Matisse: His Art and His Public*, New York, 1951, p. 105.
[4] Otto Grautoff, «Die Sammlung Serge Stschukin in Moskau», *Kunst und Künstler*, 1919, p. 83.

not know how to look at things. He loved to say, with a wave of the hand: 'Good pictures are cheap.' He was right [...] for, both from the point of view of money and of one's pride it is more interesting to buy something for three hundred francs which is soon to be worth one hundred thousand."[5]

This is borne out by a bill dated April 29, 1909 that Vollard sent, it is true, not to Shchukin but to Morozov, for fifty thousand francs, the value of paintings by various masters. The bill began with a painting by Cézanne, *Girl at the Piano*, which was valued at twenty thousand francs, three canvases by Gauguin worth eight thousand each, one Puy worth one thousand two hundred, a Degas pastel worth four and a half thousand and Picasso's *Strolling Acrobats* valued at only three hundred francs.

The different taste and temperament of Shchukin and Morozov naturally influenced their collections. Nevertheless, when we look back on the past, much that distinguished the two men recedes into the background, and we see instead the common links that bound them. Both collectors concentrated on the new spirit in French painting, acquiring works most representative of this spirit. This is the main point. Thus, the singleness of purpose shown by each collector did not make their work contradictory but, on the contrary, complementary. The common characteristic underlying both collections played a great role in their further development.

After the October Revolution a far-going reorganization of Russian museums took place. Artistic works in the great private collections which were of national interest became the property of the state and were administered by the People's Commissariat for Education (Narkompros). In 1918, the Shchukin and Morozov collections were nationalized, and a Museum of Modern Western Art opened: a museum which was to go through many stages before it reached its final form.

The Shchukin Gallery was nationalized by a decree of November 5, 1918, which specially stressed the great artistic importance of the collection. This decree stated: "Since the Art Gallery of Sergei Ivanovich Shchukin is an exclusive collection of the great European masters, especially French, of the late nineteenth and early twentieth centuries, and since, because of its great artistic value, it is of great national importance for the people's culture, the Council of People's Commissars have decreed... that it shall count as the State property of the Russian Soviet Federated Socialist Republic and shall come under the administration of the People's Commissariat for Education..."[6] The decree was signed by Lenin. On December 19th of the same year the Morozov collection was also nationalized.

At first the two collections existed as two separate museums, but they were later fused into one, although they were still housed in separate premises. Finally, in 1927, they were brought together in the same gallery, the Shchukin collection being moved to the old Morozov town house in Kropotkin Street (formerly Prechistenka Street).

When the collections had been nationalized, the work of the museum was directed by Boris Ternovets, a widely cultured man who was himself a painter and a sculptor. Besides being an outstanding art critic, he was also a brilliant organizer. He had studied painting with Yuon in Moscow and with Hollósy in Munich, and sculpture with Bourdelle in Paris. The fact that he himself was a painter and sculptor had an excellent influence on all his

[5] See Игорь Грабарь, *Моя жизнь. Автомонография* [Igor Grabar, *My Life. Automonograph*], Moscow, 1937, p. 246.

[6] See О национализации галереи Щукина. Декрет 851, «Собрание узаконений и распоряжений Рабочего и Крестьянского правительства», 10 ноября 1918 г., № 81 [On the Nationalization of Shchukin's Gallery, Decree No. 851, *Laws and Decrees of the Workers' and Peasants' Government*].

literary and organizational work; he always showed a deep understanding of art, which is so essential to anyone working in this field. His versatile nature developed quickly in the years following the revolution. This was a time of reconstruction, of reorganization, and the formation of new art institutions. As director of the museum Ternovets accomplished a great deal of creative, social and pedagogical work. It was he who welded the two very different collections into one important one.

During these years the main task of the new museum was to achieve some kind of unity in its exhibits. In 1925 the collection of Mikhail Morozov, which had been in the Tretyakov Gallery since 1910, was moved to the new museum together with a number of interesting works taken from various reserves and other collections. Thus, in these early years, many new paintings were added to the museum, including works by Edouard Manet, Renoir, Degas, Monet, Pissarro, Jongkind, Van Gogh, Carrière, Vallotton, Maurice Denis, Valtat, Toulouse-Lautrec, Forain, Van Dongen, Le Fauconnier, Rouault, Mary Cassatt, Gustave Moreau, as well as sculpture pieces by Rodin and Bourdelle.

The second task was to reorganize the hanging of the pictures. Naturally, the composition of any private collection that has been assembled with taste and understanding has its own particular charm, its stamp of intimacy and of the owner's love for his acquisitions. This quality was particularly evident in the way that Shchukin and Morozov had hung their collections in the rooms of their town houses. But if a collection is of such value as to acquire world importance, then the "private" character of the way it is hung becomes inadvisable. Making a private collection into a national museum does not merely mean opening it to the public; the paintings must be so disposed as to show the development of art during a certain period, the interaction of various trends, the evolution of different painters. The organizers of the new museum also had to take into account the fact that it was being visited by more and more people in those early years, people who were perhaps inexperienced, but who were moved by the desire to understand art. In a memorandum dated 1918, Ternovets wrote that the main aim of the new exhibition was "to bring art closer to the people". At the same time the collection was being systematically enriched. This work continually gained in scope; new departments were set up, devoted to the art of Germany, Belgium and other European countries, and a large number of new works were added to the French department.

In 1929 the museum housed a big temporary exhibition of modern French painting, which was sent specially from France, and works by Utrillo, Ozenfant and Survage were bought from it. Ternovets often made trips to Paris with the aim of adding more works to the museum. Among other things, he bought a composition by Léger, a 1925 landscape by Vlaminck, as well as a number of drawings, including some by Boudin, Léger, Gromaire, and Cocteau.

In the late twenties and early thirties the composition of the collections underwent substantial changes, brought about by the overall plans for reorganizing all the art museums in Moscow and Leningrad. In the twenties the National Museum of Fine Arts (now the Pushkin Museum) was formed in Moscow; in it were rolled into one the Rumiantsev Museum collection, the collection of Western European art then housed in the Tretyakov Gallery, and various other collections. Paintings by old masters were comparatively few and many of the best painters were missing. On the other hand, the Western European department of the Hermitage, which had been set up after the revolution and included especially French painting of the nineteenth century, stopped short at the Barbizon School and showed no examples of the later development of French painting. It was therefore decided to make changes in the three galleries. The Hermitage sent the Pushkin Museum in Moscow a large part of its collection of old masters, among them works by Rembrandt, Rubens and Poussin, while the Museum of Modern Western Art sent the Hermitage a large collection of works dating from the latter half of the nineteenth century and the beginning of the twentieth. At the end of the Great Patriotic War of 1941—45 it was decided to build up the collections of modern art in both these museums, the pictures remaining in the old Moscow Museum of Modern Western Art being divided up between them. The wealth and the high quality of the Russian collections of modern French painting enabled both museums to set up departments of French painting that are among the best in the world.

Naturally, even the finest collections of art must have some gaps: this is true of the Hermitage, too. The Pre-Impressionist period is represented rather poorly, by occasional works of Lépine, Boudin, and Fantin-Latour; especially vexing is a lack of works by Edouard Manet. The crayon *Portrait of Mme Guillaumet* in the graphic arts section, acquired in 1946, cannot, despite its exceptional quality, fill this gap. The first stage in the development of modern painting, which is linked with the birth of Impressionism, can be seen in the *Lady in the Garden* which Claude Monet painted in 1867. Here a new attitude to light and colour is to be seen alongside methods of composition used by the Pre-Impressionist landscape painters. The same characteristics are shown in *Village on the Seine*, which Sisley painted in 1872. Especially interesting are two large decorative pictures by Monet, painted in the Hoschedé garden in 1876. At this time Monet had turned away from the problem of large compositions which had interested him during the sixties, and the two Hermitage paintings, *The Pond at Montgeron* and *Corner of the Garden at Montgeron* (together with another painting of this series which is in the Louvre), are exceptions among his works of the seventies. In general the Hermitage paintings by Monet and Sisley belong to the latter period of Impressionism. Monet's pictures *Poppy Field*, *Meadows at Giverny* and *Steep Cliffs near Dieppe* show how he gradually turned his attention to capturing light and atmosphere, how with increasing sensitivity he expressed the vibrating, iridescent tones of the sun-soaked air. This motif was to become the essence of his later works, for example, *Waterloo Bridge* (1903).

A favourite theme of the Impressionists was the modern city: in it they displayed their extraordinary ability to catch a fleeting movement, whether it was a seething crowd scene, or a coach flashing by. This is the mood of Camille Pissarro's two paintings, *Boulevard Montmartre* and *La Place du Théâtre-Français*. Painted at the turn of the century, these two canvases show how, after being temporarily attracted by Divisionism, the artist came back to Impressionism at the end of his life, when he was at the height of his activity.

The small group of six paintings by Renoir is interesting because it reveals the various aspects of the artist's work. The *Lady in Black* and *Head of a Woman* were painted in mid-seventies and are typical of Impressionism. The *Portrait of the Actress Jeanne Samary* which was hung in the Salon of 1879 bears, despite its enchanting spontaneity, the imprint of Salon "showiness" which influenced the painter at that time. The extraordinary brightness of colour in *Girl with a Fan* (1881) testifies that Renoir is moving away from the strict adherence to the purely visual imprint which the Impressionists held so dear, and in the painting *Child with a Whip* (1885), the clear-cut lines of the face and the immobility of the pose betray the search for a greater stability of form typical for his works of the eighties.

Most of the Hermitage pastels and drawings of Edgar Degas are devoted to what, during his later years, became the artist's favourite theme, namely, women at their toilet. One of the finest is the big pastel called *After the Bath*, in which Degas achieves a fine harmony of feeling for line and colour.

13

Not all the Post-Impressionists are fully represented in the Hermitage. Unfortunately there are no works by Seurat. Neo-Impressionism is exemplified by Signac's landscape *Harbour at Marseilles*, which, however, can hardly be counted among the artist's best works, and by Cross' *View of the Church of Santa Maria degli Angeli near Assisi*. The latter is a fine example of the new decorative method of building up a composition which was to be developed so widely in French painting of the following period.

Despite their excellent quality, the four Hermitage Van Goghs do not give an exhaustive idea of this artist's work. Two of them, *The Arena at Arles* and *Ladies of Arles*, belong to the period when Van Gogh was temporarily attracted by the principles of synthetic painting which Gauguin and Bernard elaborated at Pont-Aven. On the other hand, *Lilac Bush*, which Van Gogh painted on arriving at the sanitarium of Saint-Rémy, can be considered as one of the finest examples of his mature style, while *Thatched Cottages* is typical of his work at Auvers, in the last tragic days of his life.

The Hermitage contains a much more complete collection of the other Post-Impressionists. There are eleven works by Cézanne which illustrate the evolution of his art, beginning with the early composition *Girl at the Piano*, with its sober colouring, and ending with the *Blue Landscape*, a brilliant piece in his mature manner. Two pictures, *Bouquet of Flowers in a Vase* and *Self-portrait*, belong to the period when Cézanne lived at Auvers et Pontoise and worked beside Pissarro, becoming aware of the achievements of Impressionism. The formation of his unique style, the elaboration of his method of painting based on the unity of colour and form and on new notions of composition can be seen from such extremely important works as *Pine Tree near Aix*, *The Smoker*, *Still Life with Drapery*, and the magnificent landscape, *Mount Sainte-Victoire*. This painting has all the splendour and dynamism of Cézanne's last works, imbued as it is with his own understanding of the cosmic forces of nature.

The Hermitage contains fifteen works by Gauguin which all belong to his Tahiti period, except for *Sweet Dreams* which he painted in Paris between his two stays in the Pacific Islands. Paintings such as *Tahitian Pastoral Scenes*, *Woman Holding a Fruit*, *The Idol* and *Motherhood*, show that Gauguin, away from Europe, worked with great force of character to perfect his sharply distinctive manner and drew freely from new sources of inspiration linked to the artistic traditions of the East.

Unfortunately, the Hermitage contains few examples of the work of the so-called Nabi group. There is one Vuillard (*The Room*, 1893), a painting whose dulled colouring creates the mood of lyrical intimacy, and four canvases by Maurice Denis, *Mother and Child*, *Christ Visiting Martha and Mary*, *Sacred Grove*, and *Wedding Procession*, demonstrating the peculiar stylization of form typical of that artist. But these alone cannot of course give an adequate idea of the work of the Nabi group, active from the late eighties. On the other hand, the Hermitage possesses some more mature works of the Nabis, when each artist had gone his own way. Denis produced decorative compositions of a somewhat eclectic classicism, such as the series of panels devoted to *The Story of Psyche*, which he did for the big salon in Morozov's house. As for Bonnard, the Hermitage possesses some excellent works produced by this outstanding painter in the early years of the century. These are *Evening in Paris* and *Morning in Paris* (1911), and also a large triptych, *The Mediterranean* (1910), in which Impressionist elements are to be found side by side with a more decorative approach to painting.

The Matisse collection of the Hermitage is particularly important, covering works from the turn of the century to the beginning of World War I. There are early still lifes, such as *Fruit and Coffee-pot*, painted when Matisse was still under the influence of Impressionism.

There are also pictures from what is sometimes called his "pre-Fauve" period, *The Luxembourg Gardens* and *Dishes and Fruit*, which show his daring search for an intense colour range and simplification of form, which were later to underlie all his Fauve works. The Museum also houses many splendid pictures dating from the height of his creative period, such as *The Red Room, Family Portrait, Conversation* and *Satyr and Nymph*, two still lifes painted in Seville in 1911 and, finally, the two famous decorative panels, *The Dance* and *Music*, commissioned by Shchukin. Of Matisse's later works, the Museum has the *Portrait of the Artist's Wife* (1913) and a series of Moroccan canvases, done in delicate water-colour tones but with such force that they outshine all this artist's preceding work as a colourist.

Apart from Matisse, the other Fauves are well represented: Manguin, Marquet, Vlaminck, Valtat, Puy and Friesz, all of whom worked together with Matisse, fighting alongside him for a new conception of colour that perturbed the visitors to the Salon d'Automne and the Salon des Indépendants, where their works were hung.

The Picasso collection is equally extensive, covering the first fourteen years of the twentieth century. There are comparatively few works of his "Blue" and "Pink" periods, although these include such outstanding paintings as *The Visit* (1902) and the pastel *Boy with a Dog* (1905). Then come two pictures painted in 1907, *The Dance of the Veils* and *Composition with a Skull*, and a series of works from 1908 which are fine examples of the crucial turn in Picasso's work after 1906. The monumental canvases *Friendship, Woman with a Fan* and *Three Women* (a later version of the central figures in *Les Demoiselles d'Avignon*), together with a large number of still lifes, characterize Picasso's work of this important period of change.

In concluding this short review of the collection, we should like to speak of the particularly interesting selection of Derain's work in the Hermitage. First a member of the Fauve movement, then a follower of Cézanne whose principles he interpreted in an original way, Derain in the first two decades of the century painted works permeated with a distinctive and outstandingly Romantic spirit. Such paintings as *Harbour in Provence (Martigues), Lake, The Grove*, and the *Portrait of Chevalier X.*, which is remarkable for an unexpected closeness to Expressionism, are obvious reminders that his works in the Hermitage belong to the years when he was at the height of his creative powers.

The Hermitage collection of French art from the second half of the nineteenth century to the beginning of the twentieth is not limited to the pictures listed above. The aim of the present publication is to show the collection in its entirety. Besides canvases by the most distinguished masters, the album presents works by lesser known artists.

The edition does not offer a complete scientific commentary to the works reproduced: only catalogue data are given, including information on the origin of each picture and on the major exhibitions where it was first displayed (Salon d'Automne, Salon des Indépendants and others). These facts can serve as a basis for dating the pictures.

Henri Fantin-Latour	Edouard Vuillard
Pierre Puvis de Chavannes	Félix Vallotton
Odilon Redon	Louis Valtat
Stanislas Lépine	Pierre Laprade
Eugène Boudin	Jean Puy
Albert Lebourg	Henri Manguin
Claude Monet	Georges Dupuis
Alfred Sisley	Albert Marquet
Armand Guillaumin	Henri Matisse
Camille Pissarro	Othon Friesz
Pierre-Auguste Renoir	Henri Le Fauconnier
Edgar Degas	Maurice de Vlaminck
Jean-Louis Forain	André Derain
Paul Cézanne	Kees Van Dongen
Paul Signac	Georges Rouault
Henri Cross (Delacroix)	Marie Laurencin
Vincent Van Gogh	Pablo Picasso
Paul Gauguin	André Lhote
Henry Moret	Amédée Ozenfant
Henri Rousseau	Fernand Léger
Maurice Denis	Léopold Survage
Ker Xavier Roussel	Auguste Herbin
Pierre Bonnard	André Fougeron

HENRI FANTIN-LATOUR
1836—1904

Fantin-Latour was born in Grenoble. In 1841 his family moved to Paris. He started drawing at an early age, taught by his father, Théodore Fantin-Latour, who was a portrait painter. In 1850 he attended the drawing courses of Lecoq de Boisbaudran and there made friends with Alphonse Legros. From 1853 on he regularly copied works by the old masters in the Louvre, as well as paintings by Delacroix in the Musée de Luxembourg, and for twelve years lived mainly by copying. He met Degas in the Louvre in 1855, Manet in 1857 and Berthe Morisot in 1858. In 1859 Whistler invited him to visit London where through Alphonse Legros and the amateur-engraver Edwin Edwards he became associated with the artistic milieu of the English capital and in 1864 exhibited at the Royal Academy. In London he was especially popular for his flowerpieces which he began to paint in the same year. He first exhibited at the Salon in Paris in 1861, and in 1862 along with Manet, Legros, Whistler and Jongkind he joined the Société des Aquafortistes. His painting *Féérie* was displayed at the Salon des Refusés in 1863. His portrait groups, *Hommage à Delacroix* (1864), *The Toast* (1865), *Atelier aux Batignolles* (1870), *At the Table* (1872), *Round the Piano* (1885) and others, provide a rich gallery of prominent personalities of his time: the artists, poets and musicians. To these portraits may be added Fantin's many lithographs and paintings inspired by imaginative themes, which reveal his romantic passion for Wagner, Berlioz and Schumann.

1   ROSES AND NASTURCIUMS IN A VASE. 1883
Oil on canvas. 28 × 36 cm
Signed and dated below right: *Fantin. 83*
Provenance: belonged to Marie Janowska, the artist's
sister, then to her descendants in St. Petersburg.
Acquired in 1950 from A. Burliayev. Inv. No. 9675

2 FLOWERS IN AN EARTHENWARE VASE. 1883

Oil on canvas. 22.5 × 29 cm
Signed and dated below left: *Fantin 83*

Provenance: belonged to Marie Janowska, the artist's
sister, then to her descendants in St. Petersburg.
Acquired in 1946 from Dr. Janowski's widow.
Inv. No. 8698

3   NAIAD. *C.* 1896
Oil on canvas. 44 × 57 cm
Signed below right: *Fantin*
This canvas is a version of the pastel *Undine* which
was exhibited in the 1896 Salon.
Provenance: the Durand-Ruel collection; subsequent
whereabouts not known; the State Historical Museum,
1918; the Museum of Fine Arts, Moscow, 1926; the
Museum of Modern Western Art, Moscow, 1930.
In the Hermitage since 1948. Inv. No. 8906

PIERRE PUVIS DE CHAVANNES
1824—1898

Pierre Puvis de Chavannes was born in Lyons. He intended to follow his father's example and become an engineer, but at the same time he took painting lessons from Henri Scheffer. He spent two years in Italy, studying the frescoes of the early Renaissance masters; this led to his subsequent predilection for monumental and decorative art.

On his return to Paris Puvis de Chavannes worked for some time in the studio of Thomas Couture, but the strongest influences at the beginning of his career came from Delacroix and especially Théodore Chassériau. His first appearance at the Salon of 1850 passed unnoticed and it was only from 1859, when his canvas *Return from the Hunt* was accepted there, that the artist began to exhibit his almost exclusively allegorical paintings annually. In 1890 Puvis de Chavannes became a founder member of the Société Nationale des Beaux-Arts where priority was given to exponents of the academic school.

In 1854 Puvis de Chavannes turned for the first time to decorative painting, producing large canvases for the dining-room in his brother's house (*The Four Seasons of the Year* and *The Return of the Prodigal Son*).

The reputation of Puvis, however, rests largely on his mural decorations executed for numerous public buildings, including the Palais Longchamp in Marseilles (allegorical scenes on the themes of the town's past, 1868—69) and the Panthéon (*The Childhood of Sainte Geneviève*, 1876—77, and *Sainte Geneviève Guarding the Sleeping Paris*, 1897—98, from the *Life of Sainte Geneviève, the Protectress of Paris* series). He also decorated the Sorbonne (1889—93), the Hôtel de Ville, Paris (1889—93), the Palais des Beaux-Arts, Lyons (1883—84), the Musée Céramique, Rouen (1890) and the Boston Public Library (1898).

Both his paintings and his mural decorations are executed in a rather abstract and poeticized style which makes use of flat, slightly modelled figures and which is characterized by smooth outlines and a pale, chalky range of colours. It was these distinctive features of Puvis de Chavannes' style that made him a hero of the Symbolist artists and writers of the late 1880s and 1890s.

4   THE VILLAGE FIREMEN. NEUILLY. 1857
Oil on canvas. 179 × 228 cm
Signed and dated below right:
Puvis de Chavannes 1857

Provenance: purchased from the artist by P. Durand-
Ruel, 1891; acquired by D. Botkin, 1900; the Museum
of Fine Arts, Moscow; the Museum of Modern Western
Art, Moscow, 1925.
In the Hermitage since 1948. Inv. No. 9672

5   INSANE WOMAN ON THE BEACH. 1887
Oil on canvas. 74.5 × 74 cm
Signed and dated below left:
P. Puvis de Chavannes 1887

Provenance: the I. Ostroukhov collection, Moscow; the
Ostroukhov Museum of Painting and Icon-painting,
Moscow, 1918; the Museum of Modern Western Art,
Moscow, 1929.
In the Hermitage since 1931. Inv. No. 6564

ODILON REDON
1840—1916

Odilon Redon spent his youth in Bordeaux. His parents wanted him to become an architect. From the age of fifteen he began to take lessons in drawing from S. Gorin who taught him to copy English engravings and water-colours. His success in drawing strengthened Redon's desire to make a career in art. In 1863 he struck up a friendship with Rodolphe Bresdin who helped him to master the technique of etching and whose bizarre compositions developed Redon's taste for fantastic subjects. In subsequent years Redon mastered the medium of lithography under Fantin-Latour. In addition to graphics the young artist showed an interest in painting and in 1864 he enrolled at the Ecole des Beaux-Arts in Paris where he attended the class of Professor Gérôme. He greatly admired Delacroix and even copied some of his paintings. He first exhibited at the 1864 Salon (Department of Prints).

Until the mid-1880s Redon's work had been known only to a narrow circle of artists. His first album of lithographs, *In a Dream World* (1879), passed almost unnoticed; his first exhibitions (at the Salon of the review *La Vie Moderne* in 1881 and at the Exhibition Hall of the newspaper *La Gauloise* in 1882) evoked hardly any response. On the other hand, his weird, highly imaginative paintings and exquisite drawings stamped by the influence of Japanese prints were hailed by the literary Symbolists, notably Mallarmé and Huysmans, by the artists of the Pont-Aven school, including Gauguin and Bernard, and by the Nabis: Bonnard, Vuillard, Sérusier and Denis. Redon was elected President of the Société des Artistes Indépendants which was founded in 1884, and exhibited at its Salon together with Seurat and Signac.

Apart from lithographs Redon produced many pastels and paintings, especially in his later period.

6   WOMAN LYING UNDER A TREE. Study
Tempera on canvas. 27 × 35 cm
Signed on the left border: *Odilon Redon*
Provenance: the S. Shchukin collection; the Museum
of Modern Western Art, Moscow, 1918.
In the Hermitage since 1948. Inv. No. 43782

STANISLAS LÉPINE
1836—1892

Lépine's biography is not very well known. He was born in Caen and died in Paris. His art shows the influence of Corot to whom he often came for advice. He first exhibited at the 1859 Salon. The financial backing of Count Doria, an art patron and collector, saved him the effort of earning his living and enabled him to concentrate on his artistic work. Lépine took part in the First Exhibition of the Impressionists in 1874, but on that his association with them ended. However, he did belong to a group of artists who were the direct precursors of Impressionism. For his numerous landscapes he usually chose unpretentious views of Paris, its secluded nooks and corners, its narrow streets with their specific cosy atmosphere, and the banks of the Seine on the outskirts of the city.

7   LANDSCAPE
Oil on panel. 26 × 39.5 cm
Signed below left: *Lépine*
Received in 1923 from the State Museum Reserve,
Petrograd. Inv. No. 5099

EUGÈNE BOUDIN
1824—1898

Eugène Boudin was born at Honfleur, the son of a harbour pilot. From his adolescence he worked in an art supplies shop in Le Havre and drew in his spare time. The artists who visited the city, in particular Corot, Isabey, Troyon and Millet, gave him valuable help and advice. The municipality of Le Havre granted him a three-year scholarship to study in Paris. Boudin first exhibited at the 1859 Salon and then at the 1863 Salon des Refusés. On his return to Le Havre he spent many summers on the farm of Saint-Siméon, in the environs of Honfleur, together with a group of landscape painters, including Jongkind, Bazille and Claude Monet. This group is often called the School of Saint-Siméon as distinct from the Barbizon School. Boudin travelled widely in Normandy and Brittany and visited Holland, Belgium and Venice. Wherever he went, he invariably painted harbour and beach scenes with numerous strolling figures. He was fascinated by towns and seaside resorts of France — Camaret-sur-Mer, Bordeaux, Deauville, Trouville — with their humid climate and shimmering, diffused light. In the 1850s Boudin met Claude Monet and did much to help the young painter find his true artistic self. In the 1860s he frequently met Edouard Manet and worked with him in Boulogne and Deauville. In the 1870s the Impressionists, in their turn, began to exert an influence on Boudin. His landscapes of that period are filled with a constantly changing iridescent light; his palette grows lighter and the brush-strokes assume the aspect of soft, blurred patches of colour.

In 1874 Boudin took part in the first Impressionist Exhibition. He also frequently exhibited with the Impressionists later, at Durand-Ruel's galleries in Paris and New York.

8   ON THE BEACH. 1880s
Oil on panel. 23.5 × 33 cm
Signed below left: *E. Boudin*
Provenance: the N. Altman collection,
Petrograd, 1922.
In the Hermitage since 1968. Inv. No. 10028

ALBERT LEBOURG
1849—1928

Albert Lebourg was born into the family of a law official. Having graduated from the local Lycée he entered the Department of Architecture at the Ecole des Beaux-Arts in Rouen. He had a particular liking for drawing buildings and medieval ruins. In 1872 he went to Algiers for four years where he taught at the Ecole des Beaux-Arts and painted townscapes.

The chief motifs of his paintings are the banks of the Seine and views of Rouen, Paris, Honfleur, Dieppe and Boulogne.

In 1879 and 1880 Lebourg exhibited together with the Impressionists, but subsequently sent his works to the traditional Salon des Beaux-Arts and to the Georges Petit Gallery.

9   VIEW OF A RIVERSIDE TOWN
Oil on canvas. 31 × 58 cm
Signed below left: *A. Lebourg*
Received in 1948 from the State Museum Reserve,
Petrograd. Inv. No. 9280

CLAUDE MONET
1840—1926

Claude Monet spent his childhood in Le Havre. In his youth he painted caricature portraits and exhibited them in the art supplies shop in which Eugène Boudin worked at the time. By his example and advice Boudin persuaded the young Monet to become a landscape painter. After finishing his military service in Algeria Monet attended the Académie Suisse and there made the acquaintance of Pissarro and Cézanne. Later, in 1862, he entered the Atelier Gleyre where he met Bazille, Renoir and Sisley. In the 1860s the young artists frequented the Café Guerbois, a place often visited also by Emile Zola and Edouard Manet. An important turning-point in Monet's artistic career came in 1869 when he and Renoir painted La Grenouillère, a floating restaurant at Bougival. The canvases they produced marked the emergence of a new artistic movement, Impressionism.

During the Franco-Prussian War of 1870—71 Monet lived in London and was introduced to Paul Durand-Ruel, a celebrated art dealer who did much to popularize Impressionist works. In 1874, in an atmosphere of increasing hostility on the part of official artistic circles, Monet and his friends formed a group and exhibited on their own for the first time. By then they had found many supporters and admirers.

The following years witnessed the flourishing of Impressionism. Monet took part in the group's exhibitions of 1874, 1876, 1877, 1879 and 1882. In those years he created such masterpieces as *La Gare Saint-Lazare* and *La Rue Montargueil*. However, his canvases found very few buyers. Desperately poor, he went to live where life was less expensive, at Argenteuil from 1873 to 1878, at Vétheuil from 1879 to 1881, at Poissy in 1882 and at Giverny from 1883 until his death. In the late 1880s his painting began to attract the attention both of the public and critics. Fame brought comfort and even wealth. During that period the artist was engrossed in painting landscapes in series under different light effects at different times of day. In 1899 Monet first turned to the subject of water-lilies, the main theme of his later work. Fourteen large canvases of his *Water-lilies* series, started in 1916, were bequeathed by him to the State. In 1927, shortly after the artist's death, these canvases were placed in two oval rooms of the Musée de l'Orangerie in the Tuileries Gardens.

10   LADY IN THE GARDEN AT SAINTE-ADRESSE. 1867
Oil on canvas. 80 × 99 cm
Signed below left: *Claude Monet*
The lady in this painting is Margaret Lecadre, one of Claude Monet's relatives, and the garden, the Lecadre family garden at Sainte-Adresse (a suburb of Le Havre). The picture was displayed at the Fourth Impressionist Exhibition, 1879 (No. 155).
Provenance: the E. and M. Lecadre collection, Sainte-Adresse; belonged to Meunier, then to Lebas, 1880s; the Durand-Ruel collection, 1893; bought by P. Shchukin, 1899; sold by him to his brother, S. Shchukin, 1912; the Museum of Modern Western Art, Moscow, 1918.
In the Hermitage since 1930. Inv. No. 6505

11 THE POND AT MONTGERON. 1876—77
Oil on canvas. 172 × 193 cm
Signed below right: *Cl. M.*
The canvas was painted on the estate of Ernest
Hoschedé in Montgeron. It was displayed, together
with other canvases belonging to Hoschedé, at the
Third Impressionist Exhibition, 1877.
Provenance: the E. Hoschedé collection, Paris; the
Vollard collection; the I. Morozov collection, 1907;
the Museum of Modern Western Art, Moscow, 1918.
In the Hermitage since 1931. Inv. No. 6562

12   CORNER OF THE GARDEN AT MONTGERON.
      1876—77
      Oil on canvas. 173 × 193 cm
      Signed below right: *Cl. M.*

      The picture was painted on the estate of Ernest
      Hoschedé in Montgeron. It was displayed, together
      with other canvases belonging to Hoschedé, at the
      Third Impressionist Exhibition, 1877, and again
      at the exhibition of the J.-B. Faure
      collection, 1906 (No. 11).

      Provenance: the E. Hoschedé collection, Paris; the
      J.-B. Faure collection, Paris, 1878; the I. Morozov
      collection, 1907; the Museum of Modern Western Art,
      Moscow, 1918.
      In the Hermitage since 1948. Inv. No. 9152

13   MEADOWS AT GIVERNY. 1888
Oil on canvas. 92 × 80 cm
Signed and dated below left: *Claude Monet 88*
Provenance: the D. Cochin collection, Paris; the
Durand-Ruel collection, 1897; the S. Shchukin
collection, 1899; the Museum of Modern Western Art,
Moscow, 1918.
In the Hermitage since 1934. Inv. No. 7721

14   POPPY FIELD. *C.* 1887
Oil on canvas. 59 × 90 cm
Signed below right: *Claude Monet*
Provenance: the G. Feydeau collection, Paris; bought
by M. Morozov at the sale of the G. Feydeau collection
at the Bernheim-Jeune Gallery, June 14, 1902; donated
to the Tretyakov Gallery by M. Morozova, 1910; the
Museum of Modern Western Art, Moscow, 1925.
In the Hermitage since 1948. Inv. No. 9004

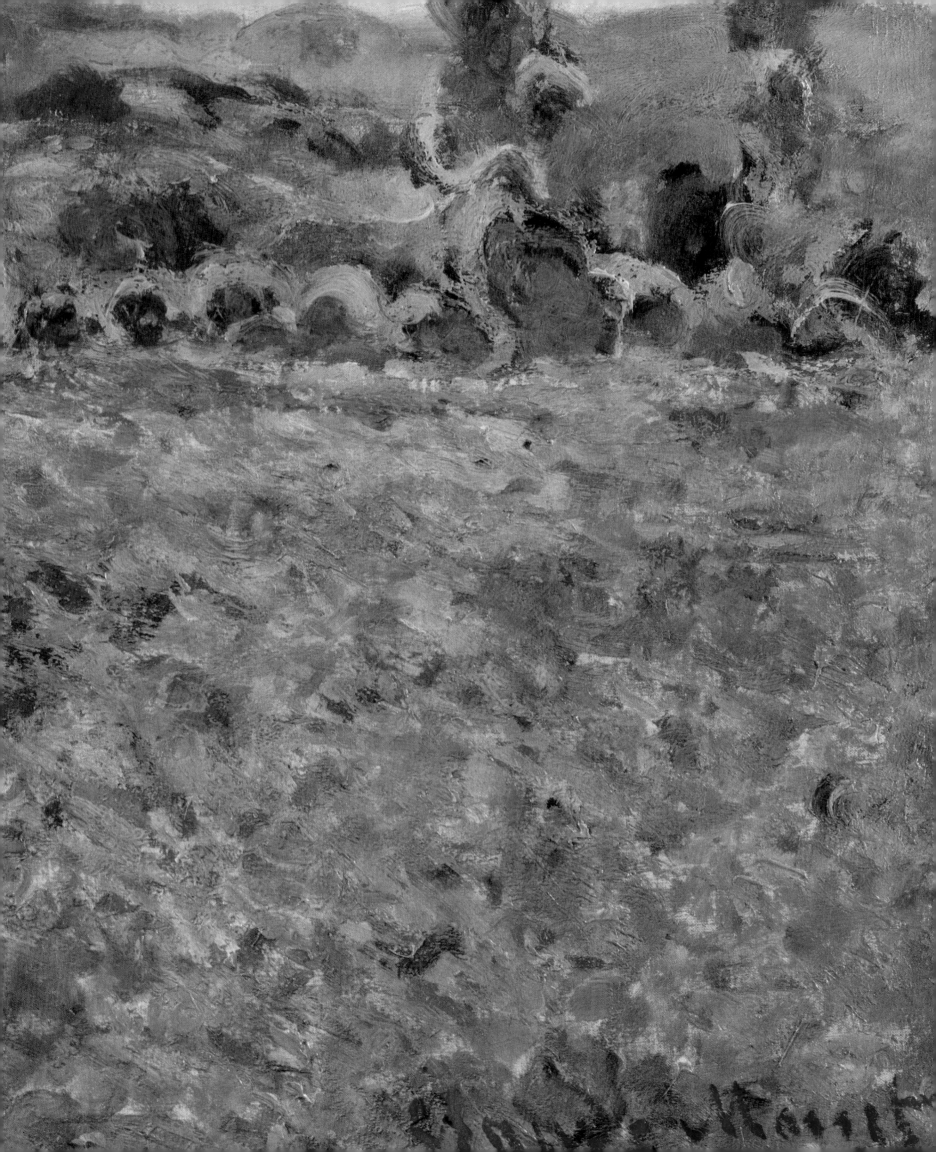

15 HAYSTACK AT GIVERNY. 1886
    Oil on canvas. 61 × 81 cm
    Signed and dated below right: *Claude Monet 86*
    Provenance: the S. Shchukin collection; the Museum
    of Modern Western Art, Moscow, 1918.
    In the Hermitage since 1930. Inv. No. 6563

16   STEEP CLIFFS NEAR DIEPPE. 1897
Oil on canvas. 64.5 × 100 cm
Signed and dated below right: *Claude Monet 97*
Provenance: the Durand-Ruel collection, 1901; the
S. Shchukin collection, 1903; the Museum of Modern
Western Art, Moscow, 1918.
In the Hermitage since 1948. Inv. No. 8992

17   WATERLOO BRIDGE (EFFECTS OF MIST). 1903
Oil on canvas. 65 × 100 cm
Signed and dated below right: *Claude Monet 1903*
Provenance: the Durand-Ruel collection, 1906;
the I. Morozov collection, 1907; the Museum of Modern
Western Art, Moscow, 1918.
In the Hermitage since 1930. Inv. No. 6545

ALFRED SISLEY
1839—1899

Alfred Sisley was born in Paris into the family of a well-to-do English businessman. Between 1857 and 1861 he lived in England where his father wished him to study commerce. Instead, he entered the Atelier Gleyre in Paris and there met Monet, Renoir and Bazille. He often worked with his new friends in the suburbs of Paris during the summer. Sisley first sent his paintings to the Salon in 1866 and subsequently exhibited there in 1868 and 1870. After the Franco-Prussian War his father was ruined, so that the artist was left in desperate poverty for many years. Until 1880 he lived and worked in the countryside and small provincial towns near Versailles and Louveciennes, especially Villeneuve-la-Garenne, Bougival and Port-Marly. The flood of 1876 at Port-Marly became the subject of a large series of his landscapes. From 1880 onwards he painted almost exclusively landscapes depicting the banks of the Seine and the Loing at Saint-Mammès and Sablon and the picturesque and peaceful life in Veneux and Moret-sur-Loing, the town where he lived since 1889 until his death.

Sisley did not live to see his talent recognized. He had contributed to the Impressionist Exhibitions of 1874, 1876, 1877 and 1882, and also exhibited at the Durand-Ruel galleries in Paris and New York. Every year, starting from 1892, his paintings were on show at the Salon des Beaux-Arts; several of his works were displayed by Georges Petit at international exhibitions. All this, however, neither brought him fame nor delivered him from financial difficulties. The failure of his retrospective exhibition at Georges Petit's in 1897, to which he had been looking forward and for which he had selected his best pictures, was an especially hard blow to the artist. Backed by one of his patrons, François Depeau, a Rouen manufacturer, Sisley left for the South of England. From May to October, 1897 he stayed at Penarth, a seaside resort near Cardiff, and painted views of rocky seashores. On his return to Moret-sur-Loing Sisley decided to apply for French citizenship. But by that time he had already become incurably ill. On January 29, 1899 the artist died.

18   VILLAGE ON THE SEINE
(VILLENEUVE-LA-GARENNE). 1872
Oil on canvas. 59 × 80.5 cm
Signed and dated below left: *Sisley 1872*
Provenance: bought from the artist by P. Durand-Ruel, August 24, 1872; the S. Shchukin collection, 1898; the Museum of Modern Western Art, Moscow, 1918.
In the Hermitage since 1948. Inv. No. 9005

19   WINDY DAY AT VENEUX. 1882
        Oil on canvas. 60 × 81 cm
        Signed below right: *Sisley.*
        The picture was exhibited at the Royal Hibernian
        Academy, Dublin, in 1904.
        Provenance: bought from the artist by P. Durand-
        Ruel, 1883; the I. Morozov collection, 1906; the
        Museum of Modern Western Art, Moscow, 1918.
        In the Hermitage since 1930. Inv. No. 6508

20   RIVER BANKS AT SAINT-MAMMÈS. 1884
Oil on canvas. 50 × 65 cm
Signed and dated below left: *Sisley. 84.*
Provenance: bought from the artist by P. Durand-Ruel, March 24, 1884; the I. Morozov collection, 1907; the Museum of Modern Western Art, Moscow, 1918. In the Hermitage since 1948. Inv. No. 9167

ARMAND GUILLAUMIN
1841—1927

Armand Guillaumin came to Paris at the age of fifteen and had to earn a living by working on the railroad. He studied painting in his leisure hours.

He met Pissarro and Cézanne at the Académie Suisse and often went with his friends to the outskirts of Paris to paint from nature. At the beginning of 1860 Guillaumin was associating with Monet, Bazille, Renoir and Sisley; he exhibited at the Salon des Refusés of 1863 and between 1870 and 1880 participated in every Impressionist exhibition, except for the Second Exhibition, 1876. In the seventies he painted almost exclusively views of the banks of the Seine, Montmartre and the environs of Paris.

In 1892 Guillaumin won a large sum of money in a lottery and in 1902 the brothers Gaston and Josse Bernheim bought some of his canvases. This allowed the artist to give up his job on the railroad and devote himself entirely to painting. He travelled all over the country and worked in Crozant and Bas-Meudon. His output — landscapes, still lifes and portraits — is uneven as regards artistic value, but the best of his pictures are distinguished by their original composition and subtle colouring.

Towards the end of his life the artist displayed a liking for bright combinations of colour, which brought him close to Fauvism.

21   THE SEINE
Oil on canvas. 26 × 50 cm
Signed below left: *Guillaumin*
On the back of the canvas is a sketch
of a river scene, and on the subframe, a pencil
drawing of a horse.
Provenance: the S. Shchukin collection; the Museum
of Modern Western Art, Moscow, 1918.
In the Hermitage since 1948. Inv. No. 8904

CAMILLE PISSARRO
1830—1903

Camille Pissarro spent his childhood and youth at Saint-Thomas in the Antilles where he studied painting under the Danish landscapist Melbye. Despite the insistence of his father who was a businessman, Pissarro refused to make a career in commerce and went to Paris in 1855. There he entered the Académie Suisse and was initially influenced by Corot. He first exhibited at the Salon of 1859 and participated in the Salon des Refusés of 1863. At that time Pissarro made the acquaintance of Manet, Whistler and Cézanne, and later met Gleyre's pupils, Monet, Sisley and Bazille. During the Franco-Prussian War Pissarro lived in London where he met Monet and was introduced to Paul Durand-Ruel. On his return to France he worked with Cézanne at Pontoise between 1872 and 1874 and took part in all the eight Impressionist exhibitions. His continual struggle to provide for his family of six children sometimes forced him to take up odd jobs, such as fan-painting.

In 1885 Pissarro joined up with the Divisionists and sent his works to their exhibitions. In 1890, however, he gave up Divisionism and returned to the freer handling of his original manner. In 1885 he settled in the village of Eragny near Gisors. During the last years of his life he often left it to stay for long periods in Paris, Rouen and Dieppe, where he painted town views from hotel windows. Pissarro did not live to see his art triumph.

22   PLACE DU THEÂTRE-FRANÇAIS. April 1898
Oil on canvas. 65.5 × 81.5 cm
Signed and dated below right: *C. Pissarro 98*
The picture was exhibited at the Durand-Ruel Gallery, May — June 1898 (No. 26).

Provenance: the Durand-Ruel collection; the S. Shchukin collection, 1898; the Museum of Modern Western Art, Moscow, 1918.
In the Hermitage since 1930. Inv. No. 6505

23   BOULEVARD MONTMARTRE. AFTERNOON SUN.
      1897
         Oil on canvas. 73 × 92 cm
         Signed and dated below right: *C. Pissarro 97*
         The canvas was painted in the spring of 1897 from
         the window of the Hôtel de Russie in Paris, and
         belongs to a series of fifteen townscapes depicting
         the Boulevard Montmartre.
         Provenance: the F. Depeau collection, Rouen;
         auctioned by an anonymous collector, April 25, 1901
         (No. 42); the M. Riabushinsky collection, Moscow; the
         Tretyakov Gallery, 1917; the Museum of Modern
         Western Art, Moscow, 1925.
         In the Hermitage since 1948. Inv. No. 9002

PIERRE-AUGUSTE RENOIR
1841—1919

Pierre-Auguste Renoir was born in Limoges and brought up in Paris, where his father, a tailor with a large family, had settled in 1845. From the age of thirteen he worked as an apprentice, painting flowers on porcelain plates and, after a mechanical method of colouring ceramics had been introduced, decorating fans and screens. Having saved some money, Renoir enrolled in 1862 at the Atelier Gleyre and there made friends with Monet, Sisley and Bazille; some time later he met Pissarro and Cézanne. He first exhibited at the Salon in 1864; after that the jury rejected his works and only in 1867 accepted the *Portrait of Lise*.

During the early period of his artistic career Renoir came under the influence of Delacroix and Manet. His Impressionist individuality was most strongly manifested in the plein-air studies of La Grenouillère at Bougival (1869).

It was in the 1870s that Renoir's Impressionism reached its peak. He worked at Argenteuil with Monet, and in Paris. He participated in the Impressionist exhibitions of 1874, 1876, 1877 and 1882 and was a founder member of the review *L'Impressionniste* (1877), where he published his treatise on the principles of contemporary decorative art.

Renoir attained renown earlier than his friends. In 1879—80 he sent several portraits to the official Salon, among them *Portrait of the Actress Jeanne Samary* (Hermitage) and *Portrait of Mme Charpentier and Her Children* (Musée du Jeu de Paume).

In the 1880s the artist found himself at a critical point. He abandoned Impressionism for what is often called the "style aigre" of painting. He began a search for solid form and stable composition, a search which led him to the masters of the Renaissance. At that time he joined up with Cézanne and worked with him in Aix, Montbriant and L'Estaque (1883, 1888, 1889). In 1885 they visited La Roche-Guyon. By the late 1880s Renoir had come a long way from the dry outlines of his "style aigre", replacing it with a free and rich pictorial style.

In December 1898 the first twinges of arthritis compelled Renoir to move to the South of France. In 1903 he finally settled in Cagnes-sur-Mer where he bought an estate named "Les Collettes", leaving it only in summer to go to Paris and other places. In his last years Renoir took up sculpture and produced some pieces of impressive simplicity. In 1912, although partly crippled with arthritis, he still continued painting, strapping a brush to his wrist.

24   HEAD OF A WOMAN. Study. *C.* 1876
Oil on canvas. 38.5 × 36 cm
Signed above right: *Renoir.*
Provenance: the Vollard collection; bought by I. Morozov, 1913; the Museum of Modern Western Art, Moscow, 1918.
In the Hermitage since 1935. Inv. No. 7714

25 LADY IN BLACK. 1876
Oil on canvas. 63 × 53 cm
Signed middle right: *A. Renoir.*
According to François Daulte, this is a portrait
of a certain Mademoiselle Anna, known as "la belle
Anna", a professional model.
Provenance: the S. Shchukin collection; the Museum
of Modern Western Art, Moscow, 1918.
In the Hermitage since 1930. Inv. No. 6506

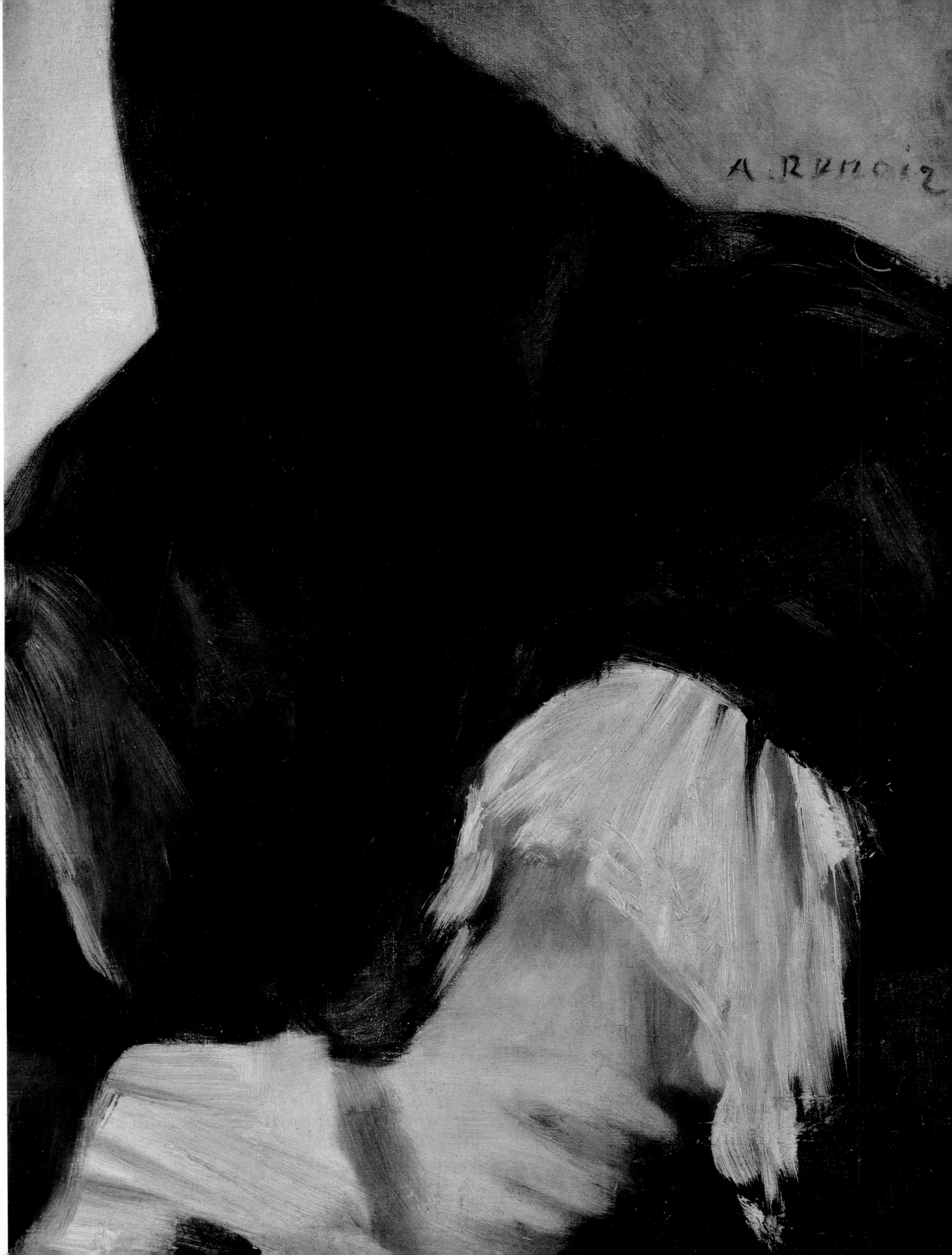
A. RENOIR

26   PORTRAIT OF THE ACTRESS JEANNE SAMARY.
1878
Oil on canvas. 173 × 103 cm
Signed and dated below left: *Renoir. 78.*
The model was Jeanne Samary (1857—1900),
a well-known actress of the Comédie-Française.
The picture was displayed at the 1879 Salon in
Paris (No. 2528).
Provenance: purchased by P. Durand-Ruel, 1879;
the Prince Polignac collection; repurchased by
P. Durand-Ruel, 1897; the de la Salles collection, Paris,
1898; the Bernheim-Jeune Gallery; the M. Morozov
collection, 1901; donated to the Tretyakov
Gallery by M. Morozova, 1910; the Museum of
Modern Western Art, Moscow, 1925.
In the Hermitage since 1948. Inv. No. 9003

27   GIRL WITH A FAN. 1881
Oil on canvas. 65 × 50 cm
Signed above right: *Renoir.*

The subject of the portrait is Alphonsine Fournaise,
daughter of the owner of the floating restaurant La
Grenouillère.

The picture was displayed at the Seventh
Impressionist Exhibition, 1882 (No. 160).

Provenance: purchased from the artist by
P. Durand-Ruel, July 25, 1891; the I. Morozov
collection, 1908; the Museum of Modern Western
Art, Moscow, 1918.

In the Hermitage since 1930. Inv. No. 6507

28   CHILD WITH A WHIP. 1885
      Oil on canvas. 107 × 75 cm
      Signed and dated below right: *Renoir. 85*.
      The subject of the canvas is Etienne Goujon, the
      son of Senator E. Goujon who ordered the portrait.
      Provenance: the E. Goujon collection, Paris; the
      Vollard collection; the I. Morozov collection, 1913;
      the Museum of Modern Western Art, Moscow,
      1918.
      In the Hermitage since 1948. Inv. No. 9006

29 LANDSCAPE. 1902
   Oil on canvas. 14 × 19 cm
   Signed below left: *Renoir*.
   This landscape depicts the artist's house at Le
   Cannet; it is dated on the evidence of the inscription
   on the back of the canvas: *Maison au Cannet*,
   and also by analogy with other works dated
   to the same year.
   Provenance: the Durand-Ruel collection; subsequent
   whereabouts not known; the Rumiantsev Museum,
   Moscow, 1918; the Museum of Modern Western Art,
   Moscow, 1925.
   In the Hermitage since 1948. Inv. No. 8926

EDGAR DEGAS
1834—1917

Edgar Degas received a sound academic training at the Ecole des Beaux-Arts under Louis Lamothe, a pupil of Ingres. As a young man, while copying the old masters in the Louvre, he met Fantin-Latour and Manet. Degas also did a lot of copying during his long sojourns in Naples between 1855 and 1859. The range of the young artist's interests was, however, certainly not limited to this. He was fascinated by Japanese prints and closely followed recent discoveries in the new art of photography.

At the very beginning of his artistic career he painted portraits, the most significant of which is the *Portrait of the Bellelli Family* (1860), and several history pictures, including *Spartan Girls and Boys Exercising* (1860), *Jephthah's Daughter* (1861), and the *Misfortunes of the City of New Orleans*, the last of which he sent to the 1865 Salon under the title *Scènes de guerre au moyen-âge*.

In the mid-1860s Degas joined up with the future Impressionists, participated in their famous soirées at the Café Guerbois, and gave himself unreservedly to purely contemporary themes. He displayed his *Steeple-chase Scene* at the Salon of 1866 and his first ballet scene, *Mademoiselle Fiocre in* La Source, at the Salon of 1868. From then on the artist turned more and more often for his subject matter to the daily life of the ballet, opera musicians and jockeys, developing a novel kind of composition based on angles of view unusual at that time.

From the 1870s onwards Degas painted in pastels more than in any other medium. In the 1880s he produced large pastel cycles of *Milliners*, *Laundresses* and *Nudes at Their Toilet*. During this period he took part in all the Impressionist exhibitions, except the one of 1882. However, the art of Degas is closer to Post-Impressionism than to Impressionism.

Besides painting, drawing and pastel, sculpture was one of Degas' constant interests, especially towards the end of his life, when his progressively failing eyesight compelled him to give up pastel.

30   AFTER THE BATH. 1884
Pastel on paper. 50 × 50 cm
Signed and dated below right: *Degas 84*
Provenance: the M. Morozov collection; donated to
the Tretyakov Gallery by M. Morozova, 1910; the
Museum of Modern Western Art, Moscow, 1925.
In the Hermitage since 1934. Inv. No. 42156

31 WOMAN COMBING HER HAIR. *C*. 1885—1886
Pastel on cardboard. 53 × 52 cm
Signed above right: *Degas*
The painting is dated by analogy with other works
of the same period.
Provenance: the Henri Vever collection, Paris;
sold by auction at the Georges Petit Gallery to
P. Durand-Ruel, February 1—2, 1897 (No. 129); the
P. Shchukin collection, 1898; bought by S. Shchukin
from his brother, 1912; the Museum of Modern
Western Art, Moscow, 1918.
In the Hermitage since 1934. Inv. No. 42154

32 WOMAN AT HER TOILET. 1889
Pastel on paper. 59 × 60 cm
Signed below left: *Degas*
The painting is dated according to Lemoisne's
catalogue (P. A. Lemoisne, *Degas et son œuvre*,
v. 3, Paris, 1946, No. 976).
Provenance: the I. Ostroukhov collection, Moscow;
the Ostroukhov Museum of Painting and Icon-painting,
Moscow, 1918; the Museum of Modern Western Art,
Moscow, 1929.
In the Hermitage since 1948. Inv. No. 43788

33   AFTER THE BATH. Mid-1890s
Pastel, gouache with traces of charcoal and varnish on three horizontal strips of grey paper pasted on cardboard. 82.5 × 72 cm
Signed above right: *Degas*
Provenance: the Vollard collection; the I. Morozov collection, 1907; the Museum of Modern Western Art, Moscow, 1918.
In the Hermitage since 1948. Inv. No. 43787

34   DANCERS. *C.* 1899
Pastel and charcoal on grey paper. 31 × 55 cm
Signed middle right: *Degas*
This pastel may have been a preliminary study for the *Dancers* in the Charles Durand-Ruel collection, Paris.
Provenance: the Vollard collection; the I. Morozov collection, 1908; the Museum of Modern Western Art, Moscow, 1918.
In the Hermitage since 1934. Inv. No. 41255

JEAN-LOUIS FORAIN
1852—1932

Jean-Louis Forain came of an artist's family and began to draw as a child. He received his early lessons in painting from Jackson de la Chevreuse, a follower of Delaroche. Forain continued his artistic training in Paris, at the Ecole des Beaux-Arts and the Atelier Gérôme. His attraction for Goya's etchings encouraged him, in 1864, to take an interest in graphics. He first scored success in 1876 when the magazine *La Cravache* published his drawings. From that time on he contributed regularly to illustrated humour magazines (*Journal Amusant, Le Rire, La Vie Parisienne, L'Echo de Paris* and others). His album *La Comédie Parisienne* came out in 1892; *Les Temps Difficiles* and *Nous, vous, eux* in 1893.

Forain also painted in oils and pastels. He exhibited at the Salon of 1884 (*In the Buffet*) and of 1885 (*A Widower*). On the insistence of Degas he participated in the Impressionist exhibitions of 1879, 1881 and 1886. Both for his paintings and drawings Forain chose subjects from daily life, depicting cafés and street scenes, the Stock Exchange or the theatres; we also find there echoes of the political events of the day. In his later works Forain's humour took on a tragic colouring, and his handling became more generalized.

35   MUSIC HALL. 1920s
Oil on canvas. 50.5 × 61 cm
Signed bottom right: *Forain*
Provenance: the H. Brame collection; bought by
P. Durand-Ruel, 1898, and sold by him to P. Shchukin
the same year; transferred by P. Shchukin's
bequest to the State Historical Museum, 1912; the
Museum of Modern Western Art, Moscow, 1922.
In the Hermitage since 1948. Inv. No. 8996

PAUL CÉZANNE
1839—1906

Paul Cézanne was born into a family of Italian origin in Cesana Forinese, at the French border, on the slopes of Mongineiro. His father had established a felt hat business in Aix-en-Provence and later became a banker. In 1859 he bought a country house on the outskirts of Aix, the Jas de Bouffan, which was to be frequently represented in Cézanne's paintings.

Between 1852 and 1859 Paul Cézanne studied at the Collège Bourbon and it was there that he formed a friendship with Emile Zola. In 1856 he began to attend the evening drawing courses of Joseph-Marc Gibert at the Aix Museum. By April 1861 his father had finally yielded to Cézanne's desire to make a career in art and allowed him to go to Paris. There Cézanne frequented the Académie Suisse, visited the Louvre, met Pissarro and Guillaumin and, later on, Monet, Sisley, Bazille and Renoir. In September of the same year he was refused admission to the Ecole des Beaux-Arts and went back to Aix, to the great delight of his father, who offered him a position in the bank. But in November 1862 Cézanne gave it up and went back to Paris.

During this so-called "dark" or "romantic" period (1862—70) Cézanne often visited Paris, meeting Edouard Manet and the future Impressionists, and trying to be accepted at the Salon. The Franco-Prussian War drove him to L'Estaque near Marseilles. Cézanne's "Impressionist" period (1873—79) is connected with his staying at Pontoise and Auvers-sur-Oise in 1872, 1873, 1874, 1877 and 1881; he worked with Pissarro and exhibited with the Impressionists in 1874 and 1877. The canvases produced at L'Estaque (1880—83) and at Gardanne (1885—88) are usually referred to Cézanne's "constructive" period.

In 1887, after a long break, he participated in the Exhibition of the Société des XX at Brussels. Towards the beginning of Cézanne's "synthetic" period (1890—1906) the young generation of artists started to take an interest in him. His first one-man show was held in the Vollard Gallery in 1895. During these years the artist seldom visited Paris — the longest sojourns there took place in 1895, 1899 and 1904 — and produced many versions of canvases depicting smokers, card-players, Mount Sainte-Victoire and bathers, and painted still lifes and portraits. By 1901 Cézanne had become recognized. He met with the Nabis — Denis, Bonnard and Vuillard. In 1901 Denis devoted the painting *Hommage à Cézanne* to him. The future Fauvist Charles Camoin sought his advice, and in 1904 he was visited by Emile Bernard, artist of the Pont-Aven school, with whom the old master corresponded extensively, stating his views on art.

In the Salon d'Automne of 1904 an entire room was reserved for Cézanne's paintings, and a year after his death, in 1907, a retrospecitve exhibition of his works was held there.

36   GIRL AT THE PIANO (THE OVERTURE TO
TANNHÄUSER). *C.* 1868—69
Oil on canvas. 57 × 92 cm
The ladies portrayed are the artist's mother and
elder sister in the sitting-room of their house,
Jas de Bouffan.
This is the most complete version of the picture.
The two other versions executed in 1866—67 have
not survived.
Provenance: the Vollard collection; the I. Morozov
collection, 1908; the Museum of Modern Western Art,
Moscow, 1918.
In the Hermitage since 1948. Inv. No. 9166

37   BOUQUET OF FLOWERS IN A VASE. *C.* 1873—75
Oil on canvas. 56 × 46 cm
Signed below left: *P. Cézanne*
Provenance: the V. Chocquet collection, Paris;
auctioned to P. Durand-Ruel at the sale of the
Chocquet collection, July 1—4, 1899 (No. 29); the
S. Shchukin collection; the Museum of Modern
Western Art, Moscow, 1918.
In the Hermitage since 1948. Inv. No. 8954

38   SELF-PORTRAIT IN A PEAKED CAP. 1873—75
Oil on canvas. 53 × 38 cm
Provenance: the H. O. Havemeyer collection, USA;
bought by I. Morozov from P. Durand-Ruel in whose
shop it had been hung for sale on a commission
basis by Mary Cassatt, 1909; the Museum of Modern
Western Art, Moscow, 1918.
In the Hermitage since 1930. Inv. No. 6512

39   FRUIT. *C.* 1879—1880
Oil on canvas. 45 × 54 cm
Provenance: the Durand-Ruel collection, 1894; the
S. Shchukin collection, 1903; the Museum of Modern
Western Art, Moscow, 1918.
In the Hermitage since 1948. Inv. No. 9026

40   THE BANKS OF THE MARNE. 1888
Oil on canvas. 65 × 81 cm
Provenance: the H. O. Havemeyer collection, USA;
bought by I. Morozov from P. Durand-Ruel in whose
shop it had been hung for sale on a commission
basis by Mary Cassatt, 1909; the Museum of Modern
Western Art, Moscow, 1918.
In the Hermitage since 1930. Inv. No. 6513

41   THE SMOKER. *C.* 1895
Oil on canvas. 91 × 72 cm
The picture was exhibited at the Salon
d'Automne, 1907 (No. 1).
Provenance: the Vollard collection; the I. Morozov
collection, 1910; the Museum of Modern Western Art,
Moscow, 1918.
In the Hermitage since 1931. Inv. No. 6561

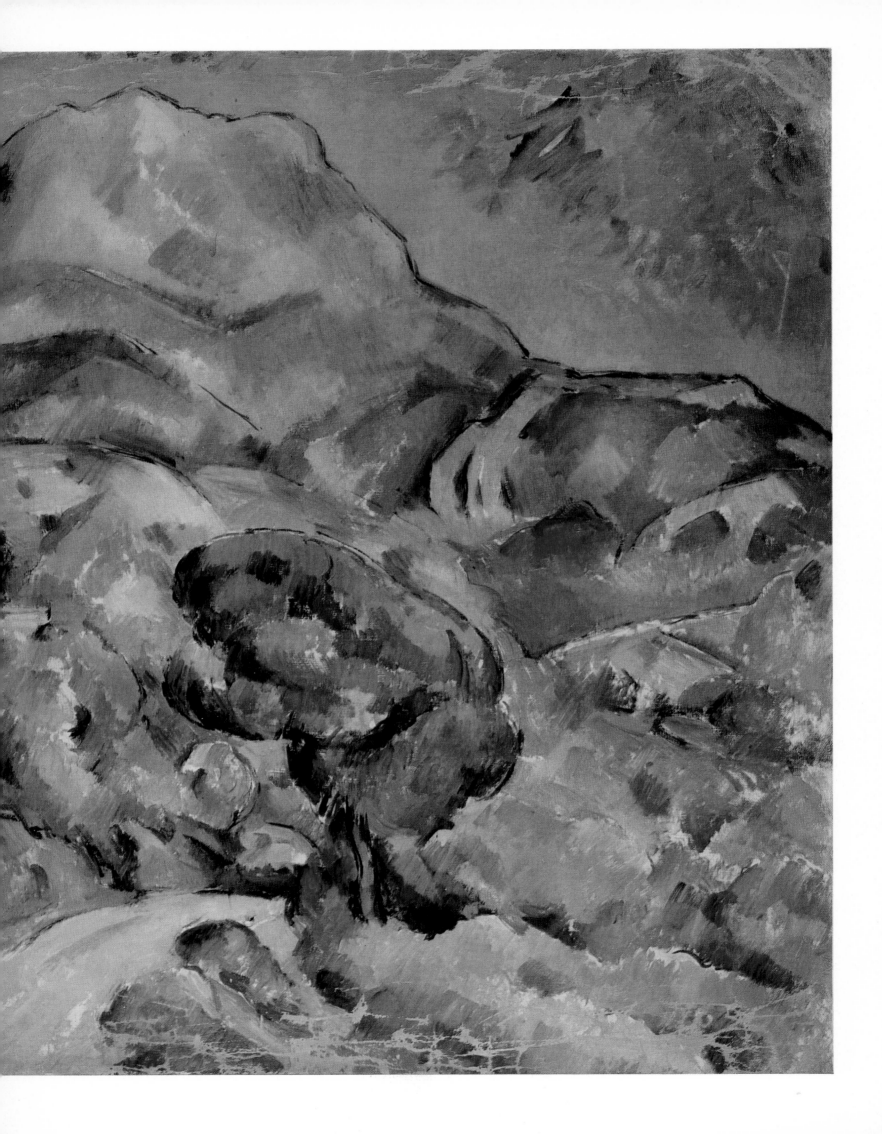

42 MOUNT SAINTE-VICTOIRE. 1900
Oil on canvas. 78 × 99 cm
The date is given according to John Rewald.
Provenance: the Vollard collection; the I. Morozov
collection, 1907; the Museum of Modern Western
Art, Moscow, 1918.
In the Hermitage since 1948. Inv. No. 8991

43   STILL LIFE WITH DRAPERY. *C.* 1899
Oil on canvas. 53 × 72 cm
Provenance: the Vollard collection; the I. Morozov
collection, 1907; the Museum of Modern Western Art,
Moscow, 1918.
In the Hermitage since 1930. Inv. No. 6514

44   LADY IN BLUE. *C.* 1899
Oil on canvas. 88.5 × 72 cm
Provenance: the S. Shchukin collection; the Museum
of Modern Western Art, Moscow, 1918.
In the Hermitage since 1948. Inv. No. 8990

45   PINE TREE NEAR AIX. 1890s
      Oil on canvas. 72 × 91 cm
      Provenance: the Vollard collection; the I. Morozov
      collection, 1908; the Museum of Modern Western Art,
      Moscow, 1918.
      In the Hermitage since 1948. Inv. No. 8963

46   BLUE LANDSCAPE. *C.* 1903
      Oil on canvas. 102 × 83 cm
      Provenance: the Vollard collection; the I. Morozov
      collection, 1912; the Museum of Modern Western Art,
      Moscow, 1918.
      In the Hermitage since 1948. Inv. No. 8993

PAUL SIGNAC
1863—1935

Paul Signac was born in Paris. He began to paint on his own in 1882 and was initially influenced by Claude Monet. In 1883 the young artist attended the free studio of S. Bing and in 1884 was among those who founded the Société des Artistes Indépendants which was to organize annual art exhibitions without jury or prizes. At about 1885 he came into intimate contact with a group of younger artists, including Seurat, Maximilien Luce, Henri-Edmond Cross and Theo van Rysselberghe, who set forth the aesthetic and technical tenets of Neo-Impressionism or Divisionism. The first canvases painted by Signac in a new manner belong to this time. Soon Pissarro joined the Divisionists, and during the formative years of Fauvism Matisse's and Derain's attention was also drawn to the technique of divided stroke.

Signac's artistic output consists mainly of seascapes and town views. He travelled widely across the country, from Le Havre to Marseilles, painting views of Paris, La Rochelle, Avignon, Collioure, Saint-Tropez and Antibes. He painted harbour scenes in Venice and Constantinople. His passion for travelling accounts to a certain extent for the specific type of his innumerable water-colours which combine a free and spontaneous portrayal of nature with a rapid, though elaborate execution. Beside paintings, travel sketches and drawings, Signac produced a large decorative canvas *Au temps d'Harmonie* for the Maison du Peuple in Brussels.

Signac has left us several important works on the theory of art, among them *From Eugène Delacroix to Neo-Impressionism*, published in 1899 and translated into Russian in 1913; a monograph devoted to Jongkind (1927); several introductions to the catalogues of art exhibitions, and many other hitherto unpublished writings.

47   HARBOUR AT MARSEILLES. 1906
Oil on canvas. 46 × 55 cm
Signed below right: *P. Signac*
Dated by analogy with a signed 1906 marine showing the same harbour of Marseilles (A. Maguy collection, Paris).
The picture was exhibited at the Salon des Indépendants of 1907 (No. 4539).
Provenance: bought by I. Morozov at the Salon des Indépendants through the agency of Bernheim Jeune, 1907; the Museum of Modern Western Art, Moscow, 1918.
In the Hermitage since 1930. Inv. No. 6524

HENRI CROSS (DELACROIX)
1856—1910

Henri-Edmond Delacroix known under the pseudonym of Cross spent his childhood and youth in Lille. At the age of ten he took drawing and painting lessons from E. A. Carolus-Duran and then studied briefly under Colas at the Ecole des Beaux-Arts. In 1878 he settled in Paris and there made friends with François Bonvin whose painting influenced him for some time. In 1881 Delacroix first exhibited at the Salon under the pseudonym of Cross, which he had chosen in order not to be confused with the little-known artist Henri-Eugène Delacroix who was exhibiting in the same period.

In May 1884 Cross took part in the first exhibition of the Salon des Artistes Indépendants and in 1891 was elected Vice-President of the Société des Artistes Indépendants. By then he had become one of the leading exponents of Neo-Impressionism. His style changed sharply. He renounced the principles of chiaroscuro and painted with rectangular divided strokes, creating canvases full of colour.

Cross often visited Italy and in 1908 he spent July and August in Tuscany and Umbria, calling at Florence, Pisa, Assisi and other Italian towns. Here he painted many studies of nature which he used for his 1909 and 1910 landscapes.

Rheumatism compelled the artist to spend his summers in the South of France; in the last years of his life he settled at Saint-Clair.

48   VIEW OF THE CHURCH OF SANTA-MARIA DEGLI ANGELI NEAR ASSISI. 1909
Oil on canvas. 74 × 92 cm
Signed and dated below right: *Henri Edmond Cross 09*
The canvas is supposed to have been painted after a sketch made during the artist's stay at Assisi in the summer of 1908.
It was included under No. 36 in Cross' one-man show at the Bernheim-Jeune Gallery in 1910.
Provenance: the Bernheim-Jeune Gallery; the S. Shchukin collection; the Museum of Modern Western Art, Moscow, 1918.
In the Hermitage since 1948. Inv. No. 8891

VINCENT VAN GOGH
1853 — 1890

Vincent Van Gogh, the son of a Dutch pastor, went to work in 1869 as a salesman in an art gallery in The Hague. He then worked in a bookshop in Holland, taught in two English schools and became a missionary in the coal-mining district of Borinage in Belgium. In his spare time he executed drawings on the subjects taken chiefly from the life of local workmen and peasants. It was not until 1880 that he decided to dedicate himself to painting. He painted his first pictures in 1881 while staying at Etten with his parents. His teacher in The Hague was Antoine Mauve.

In February 1886 Van Gogh arrived in Paris and immediately plunged into the atmosphere of the city's intense artistic life. He enrolled at the Ecole des Beaux-Arts and frequented Cormon's studio, where he made friends with Toulouse-Lautrec. Later on he met Gauguin and became enthralled by his powerful talent. He was also attracted by the light colours of the Impressionists and took an interest in Japanese prints. However, he quickly overcame all these influences and during the ensuing years his art reached its height. In 1888, while living at Arles, Van Gogh painted his *Night Café at Arles, Sower, Portrait of the Postman Roulin* and *Gauguin's Armchair*.

In October 1888 Gauguin joined him at Arles. Their cooperation was short-lived, however, lasting a mere two months, and ended in a total break and Gauguin's sudden departure on December 24.

Suffering from intermittent attacks of mental disorder Van Gogh asked to be interned at the asylum in Saint-Rémy. In May 1890 he went to live with his friend, Doctor Gachet, at Auvers-sur-Oise. There he resumed painting and produced many views of the environs of Auvers. On July 27, 1890, under the strain of mental crisis, he shot himself in the chest with a pistol and died two days later.

49 THE ARENA AT ARLES. October — November 1888. Arles
Oil on canvas. 72 × 92 cm
Dated on the evidence of Van Gogh's letter to Emile Bernard (*Verzamelde Brieven van Vincent van Gogh*, d. 4, Amsterdam, 1954, brief B. 3).
Provenance: the S. Shchukin collection; the Museum of Modern Western Art, Moscow, 1918.
In the Hermitage since 1931. Inv. No. 6529

50   LADIES OF ARLES (MEMORY OF THE GARDEN
        AT ETTEN). November 1888. Arles
        Oil on canvas. 73 × 92 cm
        Dated on the evidence of Van Gogh's letter written
        to his brother Théo in December 1888 (*Verzamelde
        Brieven van Vincent van Gogh*, d. 4, Amsterdam,
        1954, brief 562).
        Provenance: the S. Shchukin collection; the Museum
        of Modern Western Art, Moscow, 1918.
        In the Hermitage since 1948. Inv. No. 9116

51   THATCHED COTTAGES. May 1890. Auvers
Oil on canvas. 60 × 73 cm
Dated on the evidence of Van Gogh's letter
written to his brother Théo in May 1890 (*Verzamelde
Brieven van Vincent van Gogh*, d. 3, Amsterdam,
1953, brief 636).
Provenance: bought by I. Morozov through the
agency of Druet at a sale of modern paintings in
the Hôtel Drouot in Paris, 1908 (see *Catalogue de
vente Hôtel Drouot*, May 1908, No. 26); the I. Morozov
collection; the Museum of Modern Western Art,
Moscow, 1918.
In the Hermitage since 1930. Inv. No. 9117

52   LILAC BUSH. May 1889. Saint-Rémy
Oil on canvas. 72 × 92 cm
Signed below left: *Vincent*
Dated on the evidence of Van Gogh's letter
written to his brother Théo on May 9, 1889
(*Verzamelde Brieven van Vincent van Gogh*,
d. 4, Amsterdam, 1954, brief 591).
Provenance: the S. Shchukin collection; the Museum
of Modern Western Art, Moscow, 1918.
In the Hermitage since 1948. Inv. No. 6511

PAUL GAUGUIN
1848 — 1903

Paul Gauguin was the son of a Paris journalist. He lost his father in 1849. His family was forced by circumstances to emigrate to Peru, where they had some wealthy relatives and where Gauguin spent his childhood. Between 1864 and 1868 he served aboard several merchant ships, then gave up the sea and went to work for a Paris Exchange broker; he drew and painted landscapes in his leisure time. Gauguin first exhibited in the 1876 Salon. A decisive influence on the evolution of his artistic talent was exercised by Camille Pissarro whom he met in 1877. Pissarro did much to help him acquire professional skill and persuaded him to exhibit with the Impressionists. From 1883 onwards Gauguin devoted himself entirely to painting; he abandoned his business career, became separated from his family and often changed places of residence, suffering from constant lack of money. He spent the summer of 1885 at Pont-Aven and a year later embarked for Martinique.

In November and December 1888 Gauguin stayed with Van Gogh in Arles, but after a grievous quarrel this association broke up.

While living in Brittany, at Pont-Aven and Le Pouldu, Gauguin formulated the aesthetic principles of what he called "Synthesism", which were symbolic representation of nature, the use of massive, simplified forms and large, bright planes of colour. Between 1885 and 1890 eight painters grouped around him and formed the Pont-Aven school. Their first public show was held in 1889 at the Café Volpini in Paris and Gauguin's works were in the limelight. In April 1891 he undertook his first trip to Tahiti and stayed there for two years (the first Tahitian period, 1891—93). He gained nothing by returning to France in April 1893. Rejected by official critics and being in straitened circumstances, Gauguin decided to leave Europe. He set out for Tahiti, arrived there in July 1895 and settled in the north of the island. He stayed there until 1901 and then moved to Atuana in the Marquesas (the second Oceanian period, 1895—1903). During his last years, beside painting, Gauguin tried his hand at sculpture, drawing and xylography, and wrote prose pieces, among them *Noa-Noa*, *Racontars d'un rapin* and *Avant et Après*.

53 TAHITIAN PASTORAL SCENES. 1893
Oil on canvas. 86 × 113 cm
Signed and dated below right: *Pastorales Tahitiennes
1893 Paul Gauguin*
Provenance: put on sale at the Durand-Ruel
Gallery, 1893; auctioned to an unknown buyer at
the Hôtel Drouot, February 18, 1895 (No. 5); the
Bernheim-Jeune collection; the Vollard collection;
the I. Morozov collection, 1908; the Museum of Modern
Western Art, Moscow, 1918.
In the Hermitage since 1948. Inv. No. 9119

54 CONVERSATION. 1891
Oil on canvas. 62.5 × 92.5 cm
Signed and dated below left: *Les Parau*
Parau P Gauguin 91
The picture was exhibited at the Salon des Arts
Libres in Copenhagen, 1903 (No. 160).

Provenance: put on sale under No. 39 at the
Durand-Ruel Gallery, 1895; purchased by an unknown
buyer; the Vollard collection; bought by I. Morozov
with the *Landscape with Peacocks*, 1907; the
Museum of Modern Western Art, Moscow, 1918.
In the Hermitage since 1948. Inv. No. 8980

55   THE BIG TREE
(AT THE FOOT OF A MOUNTAIN). 1892
Oil on canvas. 67 × 91 cm
Signed and dated below right: *Fatata te Mouà*
P Gauguin 92

Provenance: put on sale under No. 26 at the
Durand-Ruel Gallery, 1893; auctioned to an
unknown buyer at the Hôtel Drouot, February 18,
1895 (No. 29); the Vollard collection; the I. Morozov
collection, 1908; the Museum of Modern Western
Art, Moscow, 1918.
In the Hermitage since 1948. Inv. No. 8977

56   WOMAN HOLDING A FRUIT OF MANGO
(WHERE ARE YOU GOING?). 1893
Oil on canvas. 92 × 73 cm
Signed and dated below left: *P Gauguin 93 Eu
haere ia oe-*
The inscription in Kanaka, not quite accurate,
means "Where are you going?"
Provenance: the Vollard collection; the I. Morozov
collection, 1908; the Museum of Modern Western
Art, Moscow, 1918.
In the Hermitage since 1948. Inv. No. 9120

57   SACRED SPRING (SWEET DREAMS). 1894
Oil on canvas. 73 × 98 cm
Signed and dated below left: *NAVE NAVE MOE*
P Gauguin 94
A translation of the Kanaka inscription would be
"sweet dreams".
Provenance: auctioned to Schuffenecker at the
Hôtel Drouot, February 18, 1895 (No. 23); the
Prince Wagram collection, Paris; the Vollard
collection; the I. Morozov collection, 1907; the
Museum of Modern Western Art, Moscow, 1918.
In the Hermitage since 1931. Inv. No. 6510

58   THE NATIVITY (BABY). 1896
Oil on canvas. 66 × 75 cm
Signed and dated below left: *BÉBÉ P Gauguin 96*
For the background of the Hermitage canvas the
artist utilized the composition of a picture by
Tassaert, *Inside the Manger*, a photograph of which
is known to have been at Gauguin's disposal.
The picture was exhibited at the Vollard Gallery
in 1903 (No. 28) and in the 1906 Salon d'Automne
(No. 68) under the title *Bé-bé*.
Provenance: the Vollard collection; the S. Shchukin
collection; the Museum of Modern Western Art,
Moscow, 1918.
In the Hermitage since 1931. Inv. No. 6566

59   THE CANOE (TAHITIAN FAMILY). 1896
      Oil on canvas. 96 × 130 cm
      Signed and dated below left: *TE VAA*
      P Gauguin 96
      Provenance: the M. Morozov collection; donated to
      the Tretyakov Gallery by M. Morozova, 1910; the
      Museum of Modern Western Art, Moscow, 1925.
      In the Hermitage since 1948. Inv. No. 9122

60   LANDSCAPE WITH TWO GOATS (TAHITIAN
      LANDSCAPE). 1897
      Oil on canvas. 92 × 73 cm
      Signed and dated below right: *Farari maruru*
      P Gauguin 97
      Provenance: the M. Morozov collection; donated to
      the Tretyakov Gallery by M. Morozova, 1910; the
      Museum of Modern Western Art, Moscow, 1925.
      In the Hermitage since 1931. Inv. No. 7707

61 MAN PICKING FRUIT FROM A TREE. 1897
Oil on canvas. 92 × 72 cm
Signed and dated below right: *P Gauguin 97*
Provenance: sent by the artist to Vollard in Paris,
as No. 7 of nine pictures, under the title of
*Homme cueillant des fruits dans un paysage jaune
où sont deux chèvres blanches* (Man picking fruit in
a yellow landscape with two white goats),
December 9, 1898; the Vollard collection; the
S. Shchukin collection; the Museum of Modern
Western Art, Moscow, 1918.
In the Hermitage since 1948. Inv. No. 9118

62 SCENE FROM TAHITIAN LIFE. 1896
Oil on canvas. 89 × 124 cm
Signed and dated below right: *P Gauguin 96*
Provenance: the S. Shchukin collection; the Museum
of Modern Western Art, Moscow, 1918.
In the Hermitage since 1930. Inv. No. 6571

63   THE IDOL. 1898
Oil on canvas. 73 × 92 cm
Signed and dated below left: *P. Gauguin. 98 Rave
te hiti aamu*
The artist called this picture *The Presence of the
Evil Spirit* (as translated from the Kanaka
inscription). It represents the Marquesan god Tiki or
Tikai. The picture was displayed at Vollard's Gallery,
1903 (No. 13), and again at the 1907 Salon d'Automne
where a retrospective exhibition of Gauguin's
works was held (No. 7).
Provenance: sent by the artist to Vollard in Paris
with eight other pictures, December 9, 1898; the
Fayet collection, Béziers; the S. Shchukin collection;
the Museum of Modern Western Art, Moscow, 1918.
In the Hermitage since 1948. Inv. No. 9121

64 WOMEN ON THE SEASHORE
(MOTHERHOOD). 1899
Oil on canvas. 94 × 72 cm
Signed and dated below right: *P Gauguin 99*
The picture was displayed at the 1903 exhibition
of Gauguin's works in Vollard's Gallery (No. 50).
Provenance: sent by the artist to Vollard in Paris,
as No. 8 of nine pictures, under the title of *Trois
figures*, 1903; the Vollard collection; the
S. Shchukin collection; the Museum of Modern
Western Art, Moscow, 1918.
In the Hermitage since 1948. Inv. No. 8979

65 WOMAN CARRYING FLOWERS. 1899
Oil on canvas. 97 × 72 cm
Signed and dated below left: *TE AVAE NO MARIA*
Paul Gauguin 1899
This is probably one of the studies for the big
composition *Gathering Fruit*.
Provenance: sent by the artist to Vollard in Paris
as No. 9 of ten pictures, 1903; the Vollard
collection; the S. Shchukin collection; the Museum
of Modern Western Art, Moscow, 1918.
In the Hermitage since 1930. Inv. No. 6517

THREE TAHITIAN WOMEN AGAINST
A YELLOW BACKGROUND. 1899
Oil on canvas. 67 × 74 cm
Signed and dated below right: *Paul Gauguin 99*
Provenance: sent to Vollard in Paris, as No. 10
of ten pictures, under the title of *Trois femmes
debout sur fond jaune marbré de vert*, 1903; the
Vollard collection; selected for the Hungarian
collector Nemes; the G. Stein collection, Paris;
the Vollard collection; bought from Vollard by
I. Morozov, 1910; the Museum of Modern Western
Art, Moscow, 1918.
In the Hermitage since 1934. Inv. No. 7708

67　SUNFLOWERS. 1901
Oil on canvas. 72 × 91 cm
Signed and dated below right: *Paul Gauguin 1901*
Provenance: the S. Shchukin collection; the
Museum of Modern Western Art, Moscow, 1918.
In the Hermitage since 1931. Inv. No. 6516

HENRY MORET
1856 — 1913

Henry Moret, a pupil of the history painter Jean-Paul Laurens, made his first public appearance at the Salon of 1880. He was, however, dissatisfied with the academic principles of art and joined the artists of the Pont-Aven school, who had grouped around Gauguin. From that time on Moret stayed almost for the rest of his life in Brittany where he travelled widely, stopping in small out-of-the-way villages and depicting in his many studies and sketches the Breton peasants and fishermen. But it was the rocky shores of Brittany and the endlessly changing sea views that furnished the main subject-matter for his paintings. Moret's landscapes betray a strong influence of Claude Monet.

68   THE PORT. 1896
Oil on canvas. 60 × 74 cm
Signed and dated below right: *Henry Moret. 96*
Provenance: the Durand-Ruel collection; the S. Shchukin collection; the Museum of Modern Western Art, Moscow, 1918.
In the Hermitage since 1948. Inv. No. 9054

HENRI ROUSSEAU
1844 — 1910

Henri Rousseau, called Le Douanier, came of a tin-smith's family of the town of Laval. He studied at the Lycée in his native town. In order to get away from home he joined the Army, serving as a Regimental bandsman from 1864 to 1868. After leaving the Army he married and settled in the Plaisance quarter of Paris, inhabited mostly by artisans. In 1870 he entered the customs service: hence his name. According to his own account, Rousseau received valuable advice from Gérôme and Clément. In 1884 he retired from the customs service and began painting steadily. In 1886, at the age of forty-two, he first exhibited at the Salon des Indépendants. His work of this period, however, remained unnoticed. Signac was the first to pay attention to Rousseau's naive painting stemming from primitive folk art.

Picasso, Apollinaire and Delaunay admired his talent and in 1908 organized a banquet in his honour at Picasso's studio in the Bateau-Lavoir. Rousseau was a close friend of the poet Alfred Jarry, author of the play *Ubu roi*, and himself composed music, wrote poetry and plays.

69 VIEW OF THE FORTIFICATIONS ON THE LEFT SIDE OF THE GATE OF VANVES. 1909
Oil on canvas. 31 × 41 cm
Signed and dated below left: *Henri Rousseau*
On the back of the canvas is the inscription in the artist's hand: *vue prise commune de Vanves à gauche de la porte de ce nom. Septembre 1909. Henri Rousseau*
Provenance: the S. Shchukin collection; the Museum of Modern Western Art, Moscow, 1918.
In the Hermitage since 1930. Inv. No. 6535

70   IN A TROPICAL FOREST. BATTLE BETWEEN
THE TIGER AND THE BULL. 1908
Oil on canvas. 46 × 55 cm
Signed and dated below left: *Henri Rousseau 1908*
On the back of the canvas is the inscription in the
artist's hand: *Combat du tigre et du taureau.*
*Reproduction de mon tableau exposé au Salon des
Indépendants 1908. Henri Rousseau.*

Provenance: the S. Shchukin collection, 1912; the
Museum of Modern Western Art, Moscow, 1918.
In the Hermitage since 1930. Inv. No. 6536

71 THE LUXEMBOURG GARDENS. MONUMENT
TO CHOPIN. 1909
Oil on canvas. 38 × 47 cm
Signed and dated below right: *H. Rousseau 1909*
On the back of the canvas is the inscription in the
artist's hand: *Vue du Luxembourg. Monument de
Chopin. Composition.*
Provenance: the S. Shchukin collection; the Museum
of Modern Western Art, Moscow, 1918.
In the Hermitage since 1934. Inv. No. 7716

MAURICE DENIS
1870 — 1943

Maurice Denis received a classical education in the Lycée Condorcet where he met Vuillard, Roussel and Lugné-Poë. While studying in the Lycée he took drawing lessons under Zani and copied paintings by the old masters. In 1888 he enrolled at the Académie Julian and then at the Ecole des Beaux-Arts where he attended the classes of Lefebvre and Doucet.

In the same year Sérusier showed his friends at the Académie Julian the famous landscape that he had painted at the suggestion of Gauguin at Pont-Aven and which for this reason was considered a "talisman" of Gauguin's doctrine of Synthesism. This was a decisive revelation for Denis who found himself attracted by the new ideas of Synthesism and by Gauguin's paintings which he first saw at the exhibition of the Impressionist and Synthesist Group at the Café Volpini in 1889. Denis joined the Nabis and in 1890, in the review *Art et Critique*, published his famous article in which he defined the artistic credo of the group. During this period he became associated with the Symbolist writers, illustrating the books of André Gide and Paul Verlaine's *Sagesse*, and designing frontispieces for Maurice Maeterlinck's *Pelléas et Mélisande* and for the musical scores of Claude Debussy. Like the other Nabis, Denis experimented in various fields of art, such as carpet design, painting cartoons for stained-glass and mosaic panels, and ornamentation of ceramics. In the 1890s he also did a number of mural decorations: he painted the ceiling in the house of the French composer Chausson

(1894) and executed a cycle of panels on the theme of *The Legend of St. Hubert* (1897) in the house of the collector Cochin.

His early work as a painter bears the stamp of originality, though he was strongly influenced by the art of the Italian Renaissance, especially after his trips to Tuscany and Umbria in 1895 and 1897. Despite the fact that both his paintings and mural decorations of subsequent years became rather anaemic and sugary, his fame continued to grow. The artist received numerous commissions: from 1899 to 1903 he decorated the Church Sainte-Croix at Vésinet; in 1908 he produced his *Eternal Spring* for Thomas, and in 1908—9 was commissioned by Ivan Morozov to make a series of decorative panels, *The History of Psyche*, travelling to Moscow in January, 1909, to mount them in Morozov's house. In 1913 Denis painted the ceilings at the Théâtre des Champs-Elysées; in 1917 he worked in the Church of St. Paul at Geneva; in 1924 he decorated the cupola of the Petit Palais in Paris and in 1928 painted the staircase in the Senate building; between 1936 and 1939 he did a number of decorative panels for the League of Nations at Geneva.

In addition to his work as a painter, Denis was one of the most prominent theoreticians of the time. His articles on the burning problems of contemporary art published in various magazines were later collected in two special issues: *Théories* (1912) and *Nouvelles théories* (1922).

72   MOTHER AND CHILD. 1890s
Oil on canvas. 46.5 × 39 cm
Signed below right: *MAUD*
Provenance: the M. Morozov collection; donated to the Tretyakov Gallery by M. Morozova, 1910; the Museum of Modern Western Art, Moscow, 1925. In the Hermitage since 1948. Inv. No. 8893

74 CHRIST VISITING MARTHA AND
MARY. 1896
Oil on canvas. 77 × 116 cm
Signed and dated below right:
MAUD 96
On the back of the canvas is an
original version of the same composition.
The picture was displayed
at the 1903 Sezession exhibition
in Berlin (No. 213).
Provenance: the S. Shchukin collection;
the Museum of Modern Western Art,
Moscow, 1918.
In the Hermitage since 1948.
Inv. No. 9124

73 WEDDING PROCESSION. *C.* 1892 — 93
Oil on canvas. 26 × 63 cm
Signed below left: *M. Denis*
The canvas is dated by analogy with the
1892 picture *Procession under the Trees* in the
A. Altschul collection, New York. The subject
of both pictures is connected with Denis'
marriage in 1893.

Provenance: received from a private collection
in Leningrad, 1939. Inv. No. 8342

75   ENCOUNTER
Oil on cardboard. 37 × 32 cm
Signed below left: *MAUD*

Provenance: the M. Morozov collection; donated
to the Tretyakov Gallery by M. Morozova, 1910; the
Museum of Modern Western Art, Moscow, 1925.
In the Hermitage since 1934. Inv. No. 7710

76   THE VISITATION. 1894
Oil on canvas. 103 × 93 cm
Signed and dated below left: *MAUD 94*
Provenance: the S. Shchukin collection; the
Museum of Modern Western Art, Moscow, 1918.
In the Hermitage since 1934. Inv. No. 6575

77   SACRED SPRING IN GUIDEL. 1905
Oil on cardboard. 39 × 39 cm
Signed below right: *MAUD*
The picture is dated on the evidence of an entry
in the artist's diary made in August 1905 and
describing a religious procession at Guidel
(Maurice Denis, *Journal*, t. 2, Paris, 1957, p. 20).
The title is borrowed from the 1906
exhibition catalogue of the Salon des
Indépendants (No. 1390).

Provenance: bought by I. Morozov at the
Salon, 1906; the Museum of Modern Western
Art, Moscow, 1918.
In the Hermitage since 1934. Inv. No. 7711

78   BACCHUS AND ARIADNE. 1906—7
Oil on canvas. 81 × 116 cm
Signed and dated below right: *MAURICE DENIS 1907*
The picture was exhibited at the Salon of the
Société Nationale des Beaux-Arts in 1907 (No. 376)
as the property of I. Morozov.

Provenance: bought before it was finished at the
artist's studio by I. Morozov, summer 1906; the
Museum of Modern Western Art, Moscow, 1918.
In the Hermitage since 1931. Inv. No. 6578

79   SPRING LANDSCAPE WITH FIGURES
      (SACRED GROVE). 1897
      Oil on canvas. 157 × 179 cm
      Signed and dated right (on the tree-trunk):
      MAUD 97

      Provenance: the P. Shchukin collection; bought by
      S. Shchukin from his brother, 1912; the Museum of
      Modern Western Art, Moscow, 1918.
      In the Hermitage since 1948. Inv. No. 8567

80—86 THE STORY OF PSYCHE. 1908—9

This series of thirteen decorative panels was commissioned by I. Morozov for the Music Room in his Moscow house. The first five panels were ordered in 1907 and finished in 1908, and the remaining six ordered in 1909 and finished during the spring of that year. The first part of the series was exhibited at the Salon d'Automne in 1908 (No. 531), the rest in the Druet Gallery in the summer of 1909. In the autumn of the same year the whole series arrived in Moscow.

Provenance: the I. Morozov collection; the Museum of Modern Western Art, Moscow, 1918.
In the Hermitage since 1948.

80   Panel 1: THE FLYING EROS IS STRUCK BY THE BEAUTY OF PSYCHE. 1908

81   Panel 2: ZEPHYRUS TRANSPORTING PSYCHE TO THE ISLAND OF BLISS. 1908

82   Panel 3: PSYCHE DISCOVERS HER MYSTERIOUS LOVER IS EROS. 1908

83   Panel 4: PSYCHE FALLS ASLEEP AFTER OPENING THE CASKET CONTAINING THE DREAMS OF THE UNDERWORLD. 1908

84   Panel 5: JUPITER BESTOWS IMMORTALITY ON PSYCHE IN THE PRESENCE OF THE GODS AND CELEBRATES HER MARRIAGE TO EROS. 1908

85   Panel 6: PSYCHE'S KIN BID HER FAREWELL ON A MOUNTAIN TOP. 1909

86   Panel 7: EROS CARRYING PSYCHE OFF TO HEAVEN. 1909

80

PANEL 1
Oil on canvas. 394 × 269.5 cm
Inv. No. 9666

81

PANEL 2
Oil on canvas. 394 × 267.5 cm
Inv. No. 9667

82

PANEL 3
Oil on canvas. 395 × 274.5 cm
Signed and dated below left
and in the medallion above the
bedstead: *Maurice Denis 1908*
Inv. No. 9669

83

PANEL 4
Oil on canvas. 395 × 273 cm
Inv. No. 9668

84

PANEL 5
Oil on canvas. 399 × 273 cm
In this panel Denis
portrayed his friend Aristide
Maillol as Bacchus.
Inv. No. 9670

85   PANEL 6
Oil on canvas. 200 × 275 cm
Signed and dated below left: *MAURICE DENIS 1909*
Inv. No. 9693

86 PANEL 7
Oil on canvas. 180 × 265 cm
Inv. No. 9694

87—92 SIX DECORATIVE PANELS. 1909
Oil on canvas. 390 × 74 cm (each)
Inv. Nos. 9695, 9696, 9697, 9698, 10095, 10096

KER XAVIER ROUSSEL
1867 — 1944

Roussel was educated in the Lycée Condorcet and there made friends with Vuillard. As a young boy he had been taught painting by Maillard and then enrolled at the Académie Julian where he attended the classes of A.-W. Bouguereau and J.-M. Robert-Fleury. He joined up with the Nabis in October 1888 and helped to organize their exhibition at the Gallery of Le Barc de Boutteville in 1891. He first exhibited at the Salon des Indépendants in 1901 and after that at the Salon d'Automne in 1904. In 1896 Ambroise Vollard published an album of lithographs by Roussel, Vuillard and Bonnard. Between 1896 and 1914 all three exhibited at the Bernheim-Jeune Gallery.

Roussel's early pictures are close in style to those of the other Nabis, especially of Vuillard. From 1900 onwards he developed his own distinctive manner of painting with broad sketching strokes, turning for his subjects mainly to classical mythology. His most famous decorative pieces include a series of canvases for the Bernheims (1909), several panels for the Théâtre des Champs-Elysées, which he painted with Vuillard in 1913, large decorative designs for the Museum in Winterthur, Switzerland (1915), and frescoes executed for the League of Nations, Geneva, together with Vuillard, Denis and Chastel (1936—39).

93   MYTHOLOGICAL MOTIF
Oil on cardboard. 47 × 62 cm
Provenance: the Bernheim-Jeune Gallery; bought
by K. Nekrasov in Paris through the agency of
P. Muratov, 1911; the Tretyakov Gallery, until
1925; the Museum of Modern Western Art,
Moscow, 1925.
In the Hermitage since 1948. Inv. No. 9065

94   RURAL FESTIVAL. Decorative panel. 1911 — 13
Oil on canvas. 166.5 × 119.5 cm
Signed and dated below right: *K. X. Roussel, 913*
Painted in greyish-brown mat tones in 1911, the
picture was exhibited at the 1911 Salon d'Automne
under No. 1413. After completely repainting the
picture in bright oranges in 1913 Roussel dated it
accordingly.
Provenance: the Vollard collection; bought by
I. Morozov together with the companion painting of
the same name, 1913; Museum of Modern Western
Art, Moscow, 1918.
In the Hermitage since 1948. Inv. No. 9165

PIERRE BONNARD
1867 — 1947

Pierre Bonnard was born into the family of a well-to-do official of the War Ministry, who wanted his son to become a lawyer. Shunning law lessons, Bonnard attended the Académie Julian and in 1888 entered the Ecole des Beaux-Arts which, however, he had to leave a year later after competing unsuccessfully for the Prix de Rome.

In October 1888 Bonnard joined up with Vuillard, Roussel, Denis, Sérusier, Ranson and, later, Vallotton, who called themselves the Nabis (a Hebrew term meaning "prophets"). The Nabis proclaimed that an artist should be versed in various spheres of art, the applied arts included. The group also collaborated with such eminent innovators of the theatre as André Antoine, Aurélien-Marie Lugné-Poë and the poet Paul Fort.

At the start of his career, apart from paintings, Bonnard did posters, of which the first one, *France-Champagne*, appeared in 1889; he also worked on furniture designs and textile patterns, painted screens and stage settings, and made puppets for puppet shows. His friends nicknamed him "a highly Nipponized Nabi" because his individual style of that time developed under a strong impact of Japanese prints.

Bonnard made his first public appearance at the Salon des Indépendants in the spring of 1891 and subsequently participated in its many exhibitions; in the autumn of the same year he took part in the first exhibition of the Nabis in the Gallery of Le Barc de Boutteville. In 1896 Paul Durand-Ruel inaugurated Bonnard's one-man show and in 1906 the Bernheim-Jeune firm signed an exclusive contract for the exhibition of his works. In the 1890s Ambroise Vollard published several albums of coloured prints by Bonnard and other artists and a large series of Bonnard's lithographs for *Daphnis et Chloé*.

By the late 1890s Bonnard's artistic idiom began to assume new features. He gave up sharp delineation and glaring colour contrasts for a softened spectrum based on a delicate interplay of tones. For the most part he painted landscapes, interiors and small street scenes which he saw with an artist's jovial and slightly mocking eye. The best known of his large decorative works are the reception-room panel commissioned by Missia Godebska in Paris (1910) and the triptych *The Mediterranean* done for the private residence of Ivan Morozov in 1911.

In his old age Bonnard returned to a youthful exuberance of light and colour, producing compositions of exquisite taste. During the Second World War he lived at Le Cannet in a small house called Le Bosquet, and continued living there as a recluse after his wife's death in 1942. In 1945, he paid his last visit to Paris.

95 WOMAN BEHIND A RAILING. 1895
Oil on cardboard. 31 × 35 cm
Signed and dated below left: *Bonnard 95*

Provenance: the M. Morozov collection; donated to
the Tretyakov Gallery by M. Morozova, 1910; the
Museum of Modern Western Art, Moscow, 1925.
In the Hermitage since 1934. Inv. 7709

96   DAUPHINÉ LANDSCAPE. *C.* 1905
      Oil on panel. 44 × 55 cm
      Signed below left: *Bonnard*
      Provenance: the Vollard collection; purchased by
      I. Morozov with the picture *A Corner of Paris*,
      1906; the Museum of Modern Western Art,
      Moscow, 1918.
      In the Hermitage since 1934. Inv. No. 7757

97   A CORNER OF PARIS. 1905
Oil on cardboard pasted on a cradled panel.
51 × 51 cm
Signed below middle: *Bonnard*

Provenance: the Vollard collection; purchased by
I. Morozov with the *Dauphiné Landscape*, 1906; the
Museum of Modern Western Art, Moscow, 1918.
In the Hermitage since 1948. Inv. No. 9025

98   EARLY SPRING (LITTLE FAUNS). 1909
      Oil on canvas. 102.5 × 125 cm
      Signed below right: *Bonnard*
      Provenance: bought from the artist by Bernheim
      Jeune, 1909; sold to Henri Bernstein; bought back
      from Bernstein by Bernheim Jeune, 1911; purchased
      by I. Morozov, 1912; the Museum of Modern
      Western Art, Moscow, 1918.
      In the Hermitage since 1948. Inv. No. 9106

99   LANDSCAPE WITH A GOODS TRAIN. 1909
Oil on canvas. 77 × 108 cm
Signed below right: *Bonnara*
The picture was displayed at the Bernheim-Jeune
Gallery, March 7 — 26, 1910 (No. 18).
Provenance: bought from the artist by Bernheim
Jeune, 1909; purchased by I. Morozov, 1912; the
Museum of Modern Western Art, Moscow, 1918.
In the Hermitage since 1930. Inv. No. 6537

100   LANDSCAPE WITH A RIVER (THE SEINE NEAR
       VERNON). *C.* 1910—11
       Oil on canvas. 40.5 × 51 cm
       Signed below right: *Bonnard*
       According to Dauberville, the picture should be
       dated 1906. It may have been the one displayed
       at the Centenary of French Painting Exhibition
       in 1912 under No. 42.
       Provenance: the H. Haasen collection (?),
       St. Petersburg; the I. Rybakov collection, Leningrad.
       Came to the Hermitage in 1941 as a gift of
       L. Rybakova. Inv. No. 8700

101—103 THE MEDITERRANEAN. Triptych. 1911

Oil on canvas. Central panel, 407 × 152 cm; side panels, 407 × 149 cm each
Signed and dated below middle (right panel): *Bonnard 1911*

The H. R. Hahnloser collection in Berne contains a preparatory study for the central panel of the triptych, *A Walk at Saint-Tropez*, executed in 1909. The triptych was exhibited at the Salon d'Automne in 1911 (Nos. 171, 172 and 173).

Provenance: commissioned by I. Morozov for the decoration of the staircase of his Moscow house; the I. Morozov collection, 1912; the Museum of Modern Western Art, Moscow, 1918.
In the Hermitage since 1948. Inv. Nos. 9663, 9664 and 9665

104   MORNING IN PARIS. 1911
Oil on canvas. 76.5 × 122 cm
Signed below left: *Bonnard*
A companion painting to *Evening in Paris*. It was
displayed at the Bernheim-Jeune Gallery in 1912.
Provenance: commissioned by I. Morozov; the
I. Morozov collection, 1912; the Museum of Modern
Western Art, Moscow, 1918.
In the Hermitage since 1948. Inv. No. 9107

105 EVENING IN PARIS. 1911
Oil on canvas. 76 × 121 cm
Signed below right: *Bonnard*
A companion painting to *Morning in Paris*. It was
displayed at the Bernheim-Jeune Gallery in 1912.
Provenance: commissioned by I. Morozov; the
I. Morozov collection, 1912; the Museum of Modern
Western Art, Moscow, 1918.
In the Hermitage since 1948. Inv. No. 9105

ÉDOUARD VUILLARD
1868 — 1940

Edouard Vuillard, the son of a retired captain, spent his youth at Cuiseaux (Saône-et-Loire); in 1878 his family moved to Paris. After his father's death, in 1884, Vuillard was fortunate enough to receive a scholarship to continue his education. In the Lycée Condorcet Vuillard met K.-X. Roussel, Maurice Denis and Lugné-Poë. On Roussel's advice he gave up the idea of a military career and entered the Ecole des Beaux-Arts, where he met Bonnard.

In October 1888 the future artist joined the Nabis and conributed to their exhibitions at the Gallery of Le Barc de Boutteville. He then shared a studio with Bonnard and Denis, and in 1893 designed settings and drew programmes for the Théâtre de l'Œuvre of Lugné-Poë. Vuillard first exhibited at the Salon des Indépendants of 1901 and after that at the Salon d'Automne, 1903.

In the 1890s Vuillard met the brothers Alexandre and Thadée Natanson, the founders of the *Revue Blanche*, and in 1892 did on their advice his first decorations ("apartment frescoes") for the house of Mme Desmarais. Subsequently he fulfilled many other commissions of this kind: in 1894 for Alexandre Natanson, in 1898 for Claude Anet, in 1908 for Bernstein, in 1913 for Bernheim and for the Théâtre des Champs-Elysées. The last commissions he received were in 1937 (Palais de Chaillot in Paris, with Bonnard) and 1939 (League of Nations in Geneva, with Denis, Roussel and Chastel).

In his paintings and decorative pieces Vuillard depicted mostly interiors, street scenes and gardens of Paris. Marked by a gentle humour, they are executed in a delicate range of soft, blurred colours, all his own.

106 THE ROOM. 1893
Oil on cardboard pasted on a cradled panel.
52 × 79 cm
Signed and dated above right: *E Vuillard 93*
Provenance: the P. Shchukin collection; bought by
S. Shchukin from his brother, 1912; the Museum of
Modern Western Art, Moscow, 1918.
In the Hermitage since 1930. Inv. No. 6539

107   CHILDREN. 1909
Gouache on canvas. 84.3 × 77.2 cm
Signed below right: *E Vuillard*

Provenance: the Bernheim-Jeune Gallery; the
M. Zetlin collection, Moscow; the Rumiantsev
Museum, Moscow; the Museum of Modern Western
Art, Moscow, 1925.
In the Hermitage since 1934. Inv. No. 42153

FÉLIX VALLOTTON
1865 — 1925

Félix Vallotton was born in Lausanne into a middle-class family. He went to Paris at the age of seventeen to enter the Académie Julian where he studied under Lefebvre and Boulanger. He began by painting portraits, one of which was exhibited at the 1885 semi-official Salon des Artistes Français, and then turned to interior scenes. It was in this period that Vallotton developed his own manner of painting: he worked with small, precise strokes, carefully rendering every minute detail and achieving a smooth canvas surface. This is precisely why he is regarded as one of the precursors of the so-called Neue Sachlichkeit ("new objectivity") movement which originated in the 1920s.

He first tried his hand at etchings in 1897 and subsequently produced a large number of wood engravings, quickly winning renown as a graphic artist. He contributed to many reviews, including the *Revue Blanche*, *Le Rire* and *L'Assiette au Beurre*, and designed posters.

In 1893 Vallotton broke away from the Société des Artistes Français and exhibited his picture *An Evening Swim in Summer* at the Salon des Indépendants where it was unanimously attacked by conservative critics. He also sent his works to the first Gallery of the *Art Nouveau*. By this time Vallotton had joined up with the Nabis and participated in their shows. In 1900 he was granted French citizenship and thanks to his marriage, in 1899, to a girl from the Bernheim family became a man of means. He constantly exhibited at the Bernheim-Jeune Gallery together with Bonnard, Vuillard and Roussel, and was among the organizers of the Salon d'Automne. He displayed his works at the exhibitions of the Vienna Sezession group, published his articles in the Munich review *Jugend* and the English magazine *Chap-Book*, but it was only in 1910 that he was introduced to the public in Switzerland.

In 1913 Vallotton visited Russia on the invitation of the collector H. Haasen whose portrait he completed in St. Petersburg. During the First World War the artist produced an anti-war series of drawings and painted his famous picture *Verdun*. In the 1920s he regularly exhibited at the Salon d'Automne, though his popularity underwent a marked decline.

Apart from his work in the fields of painting, drawing and sculpture, Vallotton wrote three novels and a number of plays.

108   LANDSCAPE. 1903
Oil on cardboard. 67 × 103.5 cm
Signed and dated below right: *F. Vallotton. 03*
Provenance: the H. Haasen collection, Petrograd.
In the Hermitage since 1921. Inv. No. 4908

109 INTERIOR. 1904
Oil on cardboard. 61.5 × 56 cm
Signed and dated below left: *F. VALLOTTON. 04*
The picture was probably exhibited in St. Petersburg
in 1912, under the title *La Chambre rouge.*
Provenance: the H. Haasen collection, Petrograd.
In the Hermitage since 1921. Inv. No. 4902

110   PORTRAIT OF A WOMAN. 1908
Oil on canvas. 71 × 65 cm
Signed and dated above right: *F. Vallotton. 08*
Provenance: the H. Haasen collection, Petrograd;
the Hermitage, 1921; the Museum of Modern
Western Art, Moscow, 1930.
In the Hermitage since 1948. Inv. No. 5108

111   LADY AT THE PIANO. 1904
Oil on canvas. 43 × 57 cm
Signed and dated below right: *F. Vallotton. 04*
Provenance: the H. Haasen collection, Petrograd;
the Hermitage, 1921; the Museum of Modern
Western Art, Moscow, 1930.
In the Hermitage since 1948. Inv. No. 4860

112   PORTRAIT OF H. HAASEN. 1913
        Oil on canvas. 81.5 × 100 cm
        Signed and dated above left: *F. Vallotton. 1912 + 1*
        Provenance: the H. Haasen collection, Petrograd.
        In the Hermitage since 1921. Inv. No. 4901

113   PORTRAIT OF Mme HAASEN. 1908
        Oil on canvas. 80 × 65 cm
        Signed and dated above right: *F. VALLOTTON 08*

        Provenance: the H. Haasen collection, Petrograd.
        In the Hermitage since 1921. Inv. No. 6765

LOUIS VALTAT
1869—1952

Louis Valtat was born in Dieppe. In 1880 his family settled in Versailles where he attended the Lycée and decided to make a career in art. From 1887 to 1891 Valtat studied at the Académie Julian, then at the Gustave Moreau's studio at the Ecole des Beaux-Arts. He first exhibited at the Salon des Indépendants in 1889 and subsequently, from 1903 onwards, sent his works to the Salon d'Automne. In the 1890s Valtat associated with the artists who contributed to the *Revue Blanche* and together with Toulouse-Lautrec painted the sets for the *Chariot de terre cuite* (1895). He also did drawings and woodcuts for the review *Omnibus de Corinthe* (1897).

Like many other French artists of his time, Valtat lived partly in Paris, partly in the South of France. Up to 1914 he had regularly spent the summers at Banyuls-sur-Mer, Collioure, Saint-Tropez and above all at Anthéor where in 1899 he built a house. It was in the South that he met Maillol, Renoir and Signac. In 1905 he devoted much time to sculpture (*Bust of Cézanne*, Musée Granet in Aix-en-Provence). In that same year Valtat participated in the first Fauvist exhibition at the Salon d'Automne.

During his early period Valtat was influenced by the Impressionists, Van Gogh and the Nabis. Towards the turn of the century he had already developed his own individual style. During his pre-Fauvist and Fauvist periods Valtat painted in broad, winding, passionate strokes, using strong colour effects and tending to a generalized depiction of objects and characters. In the nineteen-twenties the artist further developed this manner by outlining sharply each object, which gave his pictures a definite bias towards decorativeness.

After 1914 Valtat left the South for good and painted mostly landscapes of Normandy and Brittany. In 1924 he bought a country estate in the valley of Chevreuse, near Paris, and spent the best part of every year there. After 1948, when he had lost his sight, he was no longer able to work.

114   THE BOAT (LANDSCAPE AT BANYULS-
SUR-MER). 1899
Oil on canvas. 81 × 100 cm
Signed and dated below right: *L. Valtat 99*
Provenance: the Vollard collection; the I. Morozov
collection, 1907; the Museum of Modern Western Art,
Moscow, 1918.
In the Hermitage since 1948. Inv. No. 9109

115   LITTLE GIRLS PLAYING WITH A LION CUB.
C. 1904
Oil on canvas. 82 × 100 cm
Signed in monogram below right: *L. V.*
Provenance: the Vollard collection; the I. Morozov
collection, 1908; the Museum of Modern Western
Art, Moscow, 1918.
In the Hermitage since 1931. Inv. No. 6574

116   THE SURF (PURPLE ROCKS). 1901
Oil on canvas. 65 × 81 cm
Signed and dated below left: *L. Valtat 1901*
Provenance: the M. Morozov collection; donated
to the Tretyakov Gallery by M. Morozova, 1910; the
Museum of Modern Western Art, Moscow, 1925.
In the Hermitage since 1948. Inv. No. 8961

117   YOUNG WOMEN IN THE GARDEN. *C.* 1904
Oil on canvas. 65 × 80 cm
Signed below right: *L. Valtat.*
Provenance: the Vollard collection; the I. Morozov
collection, 1907; the Museum of Modern Western Art,
Moscow, 1918.
In the Hermitage since 1934. Inv. No. 7722

118   ANTHÉOR BAY. 1907
Oil on canvas. 74 × 93 cm
Signed below left: *L. Valtat*

Provenance: the Vollard collection; bought by
I. Morozov, 1907; the Museum of Modern Western
Art, Moscow, 1918.
In the Hermitage since 1948. Inv. No. 8887

119 IN THE SOUTH OF FRANCE. 1909

Oil on canvas. 60 × 73.5 cm
Signed below right: *L. Valtat*

The picture was exhibited at the Salon d'Automne
in 1909 (No. 1679).

Provenance: the Vollard collection; the I. Morozov
collection, 1909; the Museum of Modern Western Art,
Moscow, 1918.

In the Hermitage since 1934. Inv. No. 7718

120   SUNLIGHT UNDER THE TREES. 1909
Oil on canvas. 65 × 81 cm
Signed below right: *L. Valtat*
The picture was exhibited at the Salon d'Automne
in 1909 (No. 1684).
Provenance: the Vollard collection; the I. Morozov
collection, 1909; the Museum of Modern Western Art,
Moscow, 1918.
In the Hermitage since 1934. Inv. No. 7717

PIERRE LAPRADE
1875—1932

Pierre Laprade was born in Narbonne and made his first steps in painting under Marre. Afterwards he went to study at the Académie Carrière in Paris where he met Matisse, Derain and Chabaud. Laprade had his first exhibition at the Salon de la Société Nationale des Beaux-Arts in 1899, exhibited at the Salon des Indépendants from 1901, at the Salon d'Automne from 1906 and at the Salon des Tuileries from 1923.

Laprade was influenced by Cézanne and Renoir, but perhaps the stamp of Vuillard's "intimiste" paint-ings is most readily apparent in his art. He loved to depict gentle, blurred outlines of female figures in an interior or in a blossoming garden, and built up his colour schemes on combinations of rose, green and blue tints and tender yellows.

Besides paintings, the artist produced water-col-ours, drawings and a large number of book illus-trations, including *Manon Lescaut* by Prévost (1905), *Vers et Prose* by Valéry, *Amour et Psyché* by La Fontaine, *Un Amour de Swann* by Marcel Proust and *Madame Bovary* by Flaubert.

121   LADY IN A GARDEN
Oil on canvas. 45.5 × 73 cm
Signed below left: *Laprade*
Provenance: the H. Haasen collection, Petrograd.
In the Hermitage since 1921. Inv. No. 4904

122   LADY IN BLACK
Oil on cardboard. 55 × 46.5 cm
Signed below right: *Laprade*
Provenance: the M. Morozov collection, until 1908;
the M. Morozova collection, Moscow, until 1922; the
Tretyakov Gallery, 1922—24; the Museum of Modern
Western Art, Moscow, 1924.
In the Hermitage since 1948. Inv. No. 8985

JEAN PUY
1876—1960

Jean Puy was born in Roanne (Department of the Loire). From 1895 onwards he attended architecture classes at the Lyons Ecole des Beaux-Arts, but shortly after that began to take painting lessons; his teacher was Tollet. In 1898 he moved to Paris and entered the Académie Julian as a student of Laurens. Displeased with the traditional instruction, Puy went to study at the Académie Carrière where he met Matisse, Laprade and Derain. He had his artistic début at the Salon des Indépendants in 1901. During this period he painted in clear, bright colours, using broad, free brush-strokes, and in his creative aspirations was close to the Fauves. Puy took part in the Fauvist exhibition at the Salon d'Automne in 1905; however, as early as 1908 he broke with Fauvism.

Towards this time the artist manifested a growing preference for simplified and flat forms and more saturated colours.

In the ensuing years his art progressed but little. In his best works, Puy retained a sensuous and spontaneous feeling for nature.

Along with easel painting, he created designs for ceramics and in 1939 produced the decorative panel *Ulysses Meeting Nausicaa* for the Lycée of Lyons.

123   SUMMER. 1906
Oil on canvas. 76 × 111 cm
Signed and dated below left: *J. Puy 1906*
Provenance: the Vollard collection; the I. Morozov
collection, 1908; the Museum of Modern Western Art,
Moscow, 1918.
In the Hermitage since 1934. Inv. No. 7703

124   LANDSCAPE
Oil on canvas. 50 × 73 cm
Signed below right: *Puy*

Provenance: the S. Shchukin collection; the Museum
of Modern Western Art, Moscow, 1918.
In the Hermitage since 1948. Inv. No. 8971

125   PORTRAIT OF THE ARTIST'S WIFE
Oil on canvas. 131 × 97 cm
Signed below left: *J. Puy*

Provenance: the S. Shchukin collection; the Museum
of Modern Western Art, Moscow, 1918.
In the Hermitage since 1931. Inv. No. 7450

HENRI MANGUIN
1874—1949

Henri Manguin was born in Paris. His artistic talent manifested itself at an early age. In 1895 he was accepted at the Ecole Nationale des Beaux-Arts as a student of Gustave Moreau. There he met the future Fauves and Albert Marquet, with whom he travelled in Italy (1909) and worked at the Académie Ranson (1908—10).

In 1899 Manguin married Jeanne Carette, who afterwards posed for his pictures. He first exhibited at the Salon des Indépendants in 1902 and took part, with other Fauve artists, in the Salon d'Automne in 1905. His first one-man show was held at the Druet Gallery in 1906.

His work in Provence, in the South of France, where Manguin went in the summer of 1905, on Signac's advice, to paint from nature, was of major importance for his subsequent artistic career. It was at this period that Manguin's palette became richer and his colours, more saturated.

During the First World War the artist lived in Switzerland and there painted, among others, his still life *Flowers* (now in the Hermitage). In 1918 he returned to France.

While in his earlier Fauvist pictures Manguin resorted to emphatically vivid colours, in the 1920s he built up his colour schemes on a delicate interplay of light, soft hues. In his seascapes of that time, showing the bays of Toulon, Honfleur and Marseilles, one can discern Marquet's influence.

Subtle colour gradations are also characteristic of his works of the 1940s, when Manguin painted compositionally simple still lifes with fruit and crockery.

126 WALK AT SAINT-TROPEZ. 1905
Oil on canvas. 73 × 91.5 cm
Signed below left: *Manguin*
The picture portrays the artist's wife and sons.
Provenance: the H. Haasen collection, Petrograd.
In the Hermitage since 1921. Inv. No. 4859

127 WOMAN ON THE SHORE OF CAVALIÈRE BAY
(MORNING). 1906
Oil on canvas. 81.5 × 64.5 cm
Signed below right: *Manguin*

The woman sitting on the rocks is Jeanne
Manguin, the artist's wife.
The picture was exhibited at the Salon
d'Automne of 1906 (No. 1099).

Provenance: bought by S. Shchukin at the Salon
d'Automne, 1906; the Museum of Modern Western
Art, Moscow, 1918.
In the Hermitage since 1948. Inv. No. 8956

128   LANDSCAPE AT SAINT-TROPEZ. 1905
Oil on canvas. 50.5 × 60.5 cm
Signed below right: *Manguin*
Provenance: the Vollard collection; the H. Haasen
collection, Petrograd.
In the Hermitage since 1921. Inv. No. 4854

129 FLOWERS. 1915
Oil on canvas. 42 × 34 cm
Signed and dated below right: *Manguin 1915.*
Provenance: the H. Haasen collection, Petrograd.
In the Hermitage since 1921. Inv. No. 4955

GEORGES DUPUIS
1875—?

Georges Dupuis, born and brought up in Le Havre, received his artistic education at the Ecole des Arts Décoratifs in Paris. He won renown primarily as a draughtsman and an illustrator of books by Maupassant, Claretie and Barrès, and also as a designer of posters for a new edition of Hugo's *Les Misérables*.

After several years of stay in Paris, where he rallied to the Fauves and exhibited at the Salon des Indépendants in 1908 and 1909, Dupuis returned to Le Havre. There he lived in solitude, dropping out of the public gaze, and avoided showing his pictures to anybody. This largely accounts for the fact that Dupuis' painting remained almost unknown. For instance, Ivan Morozov, having acquired some of his canvases, took an interest in Dupuis, but all attempts by the Russian collector to discover his works at dealers' or to meet the artist personally failed.

Dupuis derived his subject matter almost exclusively from the life of the Le Havre harbour, sailors and dockers.

130 QUAI NOTRE-DAME IN LE HAVRE. 1908
Oil on canvas. 58 × 71 cm
Signed below left: *Geo. Dupuis*
The picture was exhibited at the Salon des Indépendants in 1908 (No. 2022).
Provenance: bought by I. Morozov at the Salon des Indépendants, 1908; the Museum of Modern Western Art, Moscow, 1918.
In the Hermitage since 1948. Inv. No. 8958

ALBERT MARQUET
1875—1947

Albert Marquet, the son of a minor railroad employee in Bordeaux, took an interest in painting at an early age. In 1890, he moved with his mother to Paris to receive an artistic education. There he entered the Ecole Nationale des Arts Décoratifs and then the Ecole des Beaux-Arts where he worked in Gustave Moreau's studio. At the Ecole des Beaux-Arts he met the young artists Manguin, Camoin and Matisse, all future Fauvists.

Marquet first exhibited at the Salon des Indépendants in 1901. He displayed his works at the Salon d'Automne and Berthe Weil's Gallery in 1903 and together with other Fauvists contributed to these salons in 1905 and 1906.

A close friend of Matisse, Marquet often painted from the window of his studio on the Quai Saint-Michel, doing studies and sketches of street scenes and passers-by. A desire to record instantaneously everything that caught his fancy enabled him to develop a laconic manner of drawing, reducing it to the main lines only. It was precisely the same laconic manner that Marquet subsequently attained in his paintings.

The dominant genre in Marquet's œuvre was the townscape. Since he always painted from nature, his townscapes constitute a sort of diary. He had a passion for travelling, and many of his Hermitage canvases are the result of his trips. Always preferring the seaside, he visited Menton in 1905, Saint-Jean-de-Luz in 1907 and Hamburg and Naples in 1909.

In 1934 he came to the Soviet Union, touring Leningrad, Moscow, Kharkov, Tbilisi and Batumi.

During the Second World War Marquet lived in Algiers, hardly ever quitting the country. The artist returned to France in 1945 and spent the last two years of his life in La Frette, near Paris. He died on June 13, 1947.

131 MILLINERS. 1901—2
Oil on canvas. 50 × 61 cm
Signed below right: *marquet*
Provenance: the Druet Gallery; the S. Shchukin collection; the Museum of Modern Western Art, Moscow, 1918.
In the Hermitage since 1948. Inv. No. 9030

132 MENTON HARBOUR. 1905
     Oil on canvas. 65 × 81 cm
     Signed below left: *marquet*
     The picture was exhibited at the Salon d'Automne
     in 1905 (No. 1044).
     Provenance: the Bernheim-Jeune Gallery; the
     H. Haasen collection, Petrograd.
     In the Hermitage since 1921. Inv. No. 4906

133   VIEW OF SAINT-JEAN-DE-LUZ. 1907
Oil on canvas. 60 × 81 cm
Signed below left: *marquet*
Provenance: the Druet Gallery; the S. Shchukin
collection; the Museum of Modern Western Art,
Moscow, 1918.
In the Hermitage since 1934. Inv. No. 7726

134 THE LOUVRE EMBANKMENT AND THE
     PONT-NEUF IN PARIS (TAE SUN). 1906
     Oil on canvas. 60×72 cm
     Signed below left: *Marquet*
     The picture was exhibited at the Salon d'Automne
     in 1906 (No. 1131).
     Provenance: the Eugène Blot Gallery; the I. Morozov
     collection, 1907; the Museum of Modern Western Art,
     Moscow, 1918.
     In the Hermitage since 1930. Inv. No. 6525

135 VIEW OF THE SEINE AND MONUMENT
     TO HENRI IV. *C*. 1907
     Oil on canvas. 65×81 cm
     Signed below left: *Marquet*
     Provenance: the Druet Gallery; purchased by
     I. Morozov, 1908 (under the title *Vue de Paris*,
     as in the bill); the Museum of Modern Western Art,
     Moscow, 1918.
     In the Hermitage since 1948. Inv. No. 9155

136 PORT OF HAMBURG. 1909
Oil on canvas. 68 × 81 cm
Signed below right: *marquet*
The picture was exhibited at the Salon d'Automne
of 1909 (No. 1132) under the title *Hambourg
(Soleil d'hiver)*.
Provenance: the Druet Gallery; the S. Shchukin
collection; the Museum of Modern Western Art,
Moscow, 1918.
In the Hermitage since 1948. Inv. No. 8907

137   MARINE (NAPLES). 1909
Oil on canvas. 61.5 × 80 cm
Signed and dated below right: *marquet 1909*.
The picture may have been the one exhibited at the
Salon d'Automne of 1909 under No. 1135.
Provenance: the Druet Gallery; the I. Morozov
collection, 1913; the Museum of Modern Western Art,
Moscow, 1918.
In the Hermitage since 1948. Inv. No. 9150

138   RAINY DAY IN PARIS (NOTRE-DAME).
January 1910
Oil on canvas. 81 × 65 cm
Signed below right: *marquet*
Dated on the evidence of an inscription on the back
of the canvas: *Inondation, Janvier 1910. Notre-Dame*
Provenance: the Druet Gallery; the I. Morozov
collection, 1911; the Museum of Modern Western
Art, Moscow, 1918.
In the Hermitage since 1930. Inv. No. 6526

139 PLACE DE LA TRINITÉ IN PARIS. 1911
Oil on canvas. 81.5 × 65 cm
Signed below right: *Marquet*
Dated by analogy with the compositionally similar
picture which was exhibited at the Salon d'Automne
in 1911 (No. 1057).
Provenance: the H. Haasen collection, Petrograd.
In the Hermitage since 1921. Inv. No. 4905

HENRI MATISSE
1869—1954

Henri Matisse was born at Le Cateau-Cambrésis in the North of France. He planned on a legal career, and in 1889 was employed as a clerk in a solicitor's office. It was in 1890 that he was first attracted to painting. There followed the long years of learning: in 1891 Matisse studied with Bouguereau at the Académie Julian, and in 1892 was accepted at the Ecole des Beaux-Arts as a student of Gustave Moreau, at the same time attending the Ecole Nationale des Arts Décoratifs where he met Marquet.

In 1896 he made a successful début at the Salon de la Société Nationale des Beaux-Arts and a year later displayed there his large canvas *La Desserte* which showed the influence of the Impressionists. After Moreau's death in 1898, he studied briefly with Cormon, left the Ecole des Beaux-Arts and entered the Académie Carrière where he met Derain and Puy and where he also attended evening classes in sculpture.

During his pre-Fauvist period (1899—1904) Matisse participated in a 1902 group exhibition at Berthe Weil's Gallery, painted townscapes with Marquet in Paris, spent the summer of 1904 working with Signac and Cross at Saint-Tropez, and in 1905—6 painted views of Collioure.

In 1905 and 1906 Matisse, his talent now fully developed, headed the Fauvist group, exhibiting at the Salon d'Automne and the Salon des Indépendants. At this time he displayed a tendency towards monumental decorative compositions. If in 1900 it was only to earn some money that he took on the task of painting a frieze for the World Exhibition at the Grand Palais, in 1907 he worked with enthusiasm on a ceramic triptych, *Nymph and Satyr*, for Osthaus' mansion in Hagen, Westphalia; in 1908 painted the monumental canvas *The Red Room*; and in 1909—10 executed the large decorative panels, *The Dance* and *Music*.

Sculpture, too, began to occupy a significant place in Matisse's artistic endeavour and was exhibited for the first time in 1912 in New York. At this period Matisse set forth the theoretical basis for his art in his *Notes d'un peintre* (1908), and also expounded his views on painting it the studio-school which he had organized. But soon teaching began to weigh heavily on the artist, and he withdrew more and more frequently to Issy-les-Moulineaux.

In 1910 Matisse visited Munich to see an exhibition of Islamic art, in 1911 Seville, then Moscow on the invitation of S. Shchukin, and, at the end of that year, Tangier. From 1914 to 1918 he divided his time between Collioure, Paris and Nice. In 1918 a Matisse-Picasso exhibition opened at the Guillaume Gallery; it was to a certain extent indicative of the role of these two painters in contemporary art.

In 1920 Matisse created sketches for the costumes and décors for Diaghilev's ballet *Le Chant du Rossignol* (to Stravinsky's music), and in 1939 for Léonide Massine's ballet *Rouge et Noir* (to the music of Shostakovich's 1st Symphony). In 1931—33 he painted a large decorative composition *The Dance* for the Barnes Foundation in Merion, Pennsylvania; in the same years he illustrated Mallarmé's *Poésies*. In 1934—35 Matisse produced cartoons for carpets, based on James Joyce's *Ulysses*.

During the Second World War Matisse lived in the South of France — Bordeaux, Ciboure, Nice. In 1941 he underwent a severe operation. Being confined to bed for most of the following period, he turned his attention to book design and illustration. He designed and illustrated Henri de Montherlant's *Pasiphaë* in 1944, Baudelaire's *Les Fleurs du Mal*, Mariana Alcaforado's *Lettres Portugaises* and Reverdy's *Visages* in 1946, Ronsard's *Amours* in 1948. His unique book *Jazz*, published in 1947, contained the facsimile reproduction of the text written in the artist's own hand and twenty colour illustrations executed in gouache after Matisse's *papiers collés*.

It was only after the end of the war that Matisse turned anew to monumental compositions. He executed sketches for the stained-glass panel representing St. Dominique in the church at Assy (1948), the entire decoration of the Chapelle du Rosaire at Vence (1948—51) and sketches for the stained-glass panel *Rose* for the Uniate Church in New York (1954). In his last years he devoted a great deal of his time to cut-outs and brush drawings.

The Musée Matisse was opened in 1952 at Le Cateau-Cambrésis, the birthplace of the artist. Matisse died on November 3, 1954.

140   VASE OF SUNFLOWERS. 1898

Oil on canvas. 46 × 38 cm
Signed below right: *Henri-Matisse*

Dated on the basis of stylistic features characteristie
of the artist's other paintings bearing the date
1898, notably *The Sunset in Corsica* in the
Dr. A. M. Sackler collection, New York.

Provenance: the M. Zetlin collection, Moscow; the
Rumiantsev Museum, Moscow; the Museum of Modern
Western Art, Moscow, 1925.
In the Hermitage since 1934. Inv. No. 7706

141   BLUE POT AND LEMON. *C.* 1897
Oil on canvas. 39 × 46.5 cm
Signed above left: *Henri-Matisse*
Provenance: the Druet Gallery; the I. Morozov
collection, 1908; the Museum of Modern Western
Art, Moscow, 1918.
In the Hermitage since 1934. Inv. No. 7698

142 FRUIT AND COFFEE-POT. 1899
Oil on canvas. 38.5 × 46 cm
Signed below left: *H. Matisse*
Dated on the basis of stylistic features
characteristic of the artist's several still lifes of
1899 executed in Toulouse. The inscription *Pour
M. Van de Velde* on the back of the canvas points
to the fact that the picture was originally intended
for the Belgian architect Van de Velde.
Provenance: the Druet Gallery; the I. Morozov
collection, 1910, the Museum of Modern
Western Art, Moscow, 1918.
In the Museum since 1948. Inv. No. 8892

143   CROCKERY ON A TABLE. 1900
      Oil on canvas. 97 × 82 cm
      Signed and dated below right: *Henri Matisse 1900*
      Provenance: the S. Shchukin collection; the Museum
      of Modern Western Art, Moscow, 1918.
      In the Hermitage since 1930. Inv. No. 6518

144   STILL LIFE WITH DISHES AND FRUIT. 1901
Oil on canvas. 51 × 61.5 cm
Signed below left: *H Matisse*
Provenance: the S. Shchukin collection; the Museum
of Modern Western Art, Moscow, 1918.
In the Hermitage since 1934. Inv. No. 7697

145   THE LUXEMBOURG GARDENS. *C.* 1901—2
Oil on canvas. 59.5 × 81.5 cm
Signed below right: *Henri Matisse*
Provenance: the Druet Gallery; the S. Shchukin
collection; the Museum of Modern Western Art,
Moscow, 1918.
In the Hermitage since 1948. Inv. No. 9041

146   STILL LIFE WITH VASE, BOTTLE AND FRUIT.
       C. 1903—6
       Oil on canvas. 73 × 92 cm
       Signed below left: *Henri Matisse*
       The date 1903 is given on the basis of a verbal
       statement made by the artist's daughter, Mme
       Duthuit. On the other hand, the table-cloth with
       the flower-basket pattern appears in Matisse's
       canvases only about 1906. The picture was painted
       over an earlier still life. The picture was exhibited
       at the Druet Gallery (No. 46) under the title *Camaieu
       bleu* in 1906.
       Provenance: bought by S. Shchukin, 1908; the
       Museum of Modern Western Art, Moscow, 1918.
       In the Hermitage since 1934. Inv. No. 7696

147 LADY ON THE TERRACE. *C.* 1906
Oil on canvas. 65 × 80.5 cm
Signed below left: *Henri-Matisse*
The former title, *Venice*, is erroneous. The picture
was painted at Collioure.
Provenance: the Druet Gallery; the S. Shchukin
collection; the Museum of Modern Western Art,
Moscow, 1918.
In the Hermitage since 1948. Inv. No. 9040

148   THE RED ROOM (LA DESSERTE. HARMONY
      IN RED). 1908—9. Sacré-Cœur, Paris
      Oil on canvas. 180 × 220 cm
      Signed and dated below left: *Henri Matisse 1908*
      The picture was originally executed in green tones,
      then was repainted in blues and exhibited at the
      1908 Salon d'Automne under the title of *Harmonie en*
      bleu. Panneau décoratif pour salle à manger (No. 898).
      At the beginning of 1909, prior to dispatching it to
      Moscow, the artist repainted the picture in red.
      Provenance: bought from the artist by S. Shchukin,
      1908; the Museum of Modern Western Art,
      Moscow, 1918.
      In the Hermitage since 1948. Inv. No. 9660

149   DISHES AND FRUIT ON A RED AND BLACK
CARPET. 1906

Oil on canvas. 61 × 74 cm
Signed below left: *Henri Matisse*
On the back of the canvas: *1906. Salon d'Automne.*

Dated on the basis of comparison with *Still Life
with a Red Carpet* in the Grenoble Museum.
The picture was exhibited at the 1906 Salon
d'Automne (No. 1172).

Provenance: the Druet Gallery; the S. Shchukin
collection; the Museum of Modern Western Art,
Moscow, 1908.
In the Hermitage since 1948. Inv. No. 8998

150   VIEW OF COLLIOURE. 1906
Oil on canvas. 59.5 × 73 cm
Signed below left: *H. Matisse*
Dated on stylistic grounds.
Provenance: the Bernheim-Jeune Gallery; the
S. Shchukin collection; the Museum of Modern
Western Art, Moscow, 1918.
In the Hermitage since 1948. Inv. No. 8997

151 BOUQUET (VASE WITH TWO HANDLES).
1907, spring
Oil on canvas. 74 × 61 cm
Signed below right: *Henri-Matisse*
Dated on the evidence of an inscription on the back of the canvas: *Printemps 1907*. It is also known that the vase in the still life was brought home by Matisse from Biskra (Algiers) in 1906.

Provenance: the Bernheim-Jeune Gallery; the I. Morozov collection, October 1907; the Museum of Modern Western Art, Moscow, 1918.
In the Hermitage since 1930. Inv. No. 6522

152 NUDE (BLACK AND GOLD). 1908.
Sacré-Cœur, Paris
Oil on canvas. 100 × 65 cm
Signed below right: *Henri Matisse*
Dated by analogy with the *Nude* (No. 153) and the
Woman Seated (No. 154) bearing the date 1908 in
the artist's own hand.
Provenance: the Bernheim-Jeune Gallery; the
S. Shchukin collection; the Museum of Modern
Western Art, Moscow, 1918.
In the Hermitage since 1948. Inv. No. 9057

153 NUDE. Study. 1908
Oil on canvas. 60 × 50 cm
Signed with the inscription below left: *A Monsieur
I. Ostrooukoff hommage respectueux Henri Matisse*
The author's inscription on the subframe: *Etude faite
en 1908*
Provenance: sent by the artist to I. Ostroukhov,
January 1912; the I. Ostroukhov collection, Moscow,
1912; the I. Ostroukhov Museum of Painting and
Icon-painting, Moscow, 1918; the Museum of Modern
Western Art, Moscow, 1929.
In the Hermitage since 1930. Inv. No. 6523

154 WOMAN SEATED. 1908
Oil on canvas. 80.5 × 52 cm
Signed and dated below left: *Henri Matisse 1908*
The picture was exhibited at the Salon d'Automne
in 1908 (No. 893).
Provenance: bought at the Salon by I. Morozov
through the agency of Eugène Blot; the Museum of
Modern Western Art, Moscow, 1918.
In the Hermitage since 1948. Inv. No. 9039

155   BLUE TABLE-CLOTH. 1909. Sacré-Cœur, Paris
Oil on canvas. 88 × 118 cm
Signed and dated below left: *Henri Matisse 09-*
Provenance: the S. Shchukin collection; the Museum
of Modern Western Art, Moscow, 1918.
In the Hermitage since 1931. Inv. No. 6569

156 CONVERSATION. 1909. Issy-les-Moulineaux
Oil on canvas. 177 × 217 cm
Dated on the basis of stylistic analysis.
The picture was displayed at the Grafton Galleries
(London) in October — December 1912 as the
property of S. Shchukin (No. 28).
Provenance: the S. Shchukin collection, 1912; the
Museum of Modern Western Art, Moscow, 1918.
In the Hermitage since 1930. Inv. No. 6521

157   A GAME OF BOWLS. 1908
Oil on canvas. 113.5 × 145 cm
Signed in monogram and dated below left: *H. M 08*
Provenance: the S. Shchukin collection; the Museum
of Modern Western Art, Moscow, 1918.
In the Hermitage since 1948. Inv. No. 9154

158   NYMPH AND SATYR. 1909
Oil on canvas. 89 × 117 cm
Signed and dated below right: *Henri Matisse 09-*
The composition closely resembles the central part
of the ceramic triptych executed in 1907 for Osthaus'
mansion in Hagen, Westphalia.
Provenance: the Bernheim-Jeune Gallery; the
S. Shchukin collection; the Museum of Modern Western
Art, Moscow, 1918.
In the Hermitage since 1948. Inv. No. 9058

159   FRUIT, FLOWERS AND PANEL *THE DANCE*. 1909
Oil on canvas. 89 × 116 cm
Signed and dated below right: *Henri-Matisse 1909*
Reproduced here is the first version of the
decorative panel *The Dance* housed in the Museum
of Modern Art, New York.
The picture was exhibited at the Bernheim-Jeune
Gallery in February 1910 (No. 64).
Provenance: bought from the artist by I. Morozov,
1910; the Museum of Modern Western Art,
Moscow, 1918.
In the Hermitage since 1948. Inv. No. 9042

160 WOMAN IN GREEN WITH A CARNATION. 1909
Oil on canvas. 65 × 54 cm
Signed below left: *Henri Matisse*
The canvas portrays the model Brouty, who sat for
the artist on many occasions during the summer of
1909 in the small town of Cavalière (Var).
Provenance: the Bernheim-Jeune Gallery; the
S. Shchukin collection; the Museum of Modern
Western Art, Moscow, 1918.
In the Hermitage since 1930. Inv. No. 6519

161   PINK STATUETTE AND PITCHER ON A RED
        CHEST OF DRAWERS. 1910. Issy-les-Moulineaux
        Oil on canvas. 90 × 117 cm
        Signed and dated below right: *Henri Matisse 10*
        Provenance: the S. Shchukin collection; the Museum
        of Modern Western Art, Moscow, 1918.
        In the Hermitage since 1930. Inv. No. 6520

162   GIRL WITH TULIPS (PORTRAIT OF JEANNE
        VADERIN). 1910. Issy-les-Moulineaux
        Oil on canvas. 92 × 73.5 cm
        Signed and dated below left: *Henri Matisse 10*
        The picture was exhibited at the Salon des
        Indépendants in 1910 (No. 5445).
        Provenance: the Bernheim-Jeune Gallery; the
        S. Shchukin collection, 1910; the Museum of Modern
        Western Art, Moscow, 1918.
        In the Hermitage since 1948. Inv. No. 9056

163   MUSIC. DECORATIVE PANEL. 1910.
Issy-les-Moulineaux
Oil on canvas. 260 × 389 cm
Signed and dated below right: *Henri Matisse 1910*
The panel was executed in 1910 on S. Shchukin's
order for his mansion in Moscow. It was exhibited
at the Salon d'Automne in 1910 (No. 537).
Provenance: the S. Shchukin collection, December 4,
1910; the Museum of Modern Western Art,
Moscow, 1918.
In the Hermitage since 1948. Inv. No. 9674

164   THE DANCE. DECORATIVE PANEL. 1910.
Issy-les-Moulineaux

Oil on canvas. 260 × 319 cm
Signed and dated below right: *Henri Matisse 1910*

The panel was executed in 1910 on S. Shchukin's
order for his mansion in Moscow. It was exhibited
at the Salon d'Automne in 1910 (No. 536).

Provenance: the S. Shchukin collection, December 4,
1910; the Museum of Mcdern Western Art,
Moscow, 1918.

In the Hermitage since 1948. Inv. No. 9673

165 THE ARTIST'S FAMILY.
1911. Issy-les-Moulineaux
Oil on canvas. 143 × 194 cm
Signed and dated on the subframe:
Henri Matisse 1911
Provenance: the S. Shchukin collection;
the Museum of Modern Western Art,
Moscow, 1918.
In the Hermitage since 1948.
Inv. No. 8940

166 SEVILLE STILL LIFE. 1911. Seville
Oil on canvas. 90 × 117 cm
Signed below right: *Henri Matisse*
On the back of the canvas is a brush sketch
of a woman's head.
Provenance: bought from the artist by S. Shchukin,
1911; the Museum of Modern Western Art,
Moscow, 1918.
In the Hermitage since 1931. Inv. No. 6570

167   SPANISH STILL LIFE. 1911. Seville

Oil on canvas. 89 × 116 cm
Signed below right: *Henri Matisse*

Provenance: bought from the artist by S. Shchukin,
1911; the Museum of Modern Western Art,
Moscow, 1918.
In the Hermitage since 1948. Inv. No. 9043

168   VASE OF IRISES. 1912
        Oil on canvas. 118 × 100 cm
        Signed below left: *Henri Matisse*
        Dated on the evidence of an inscription on the back
        of the canvas: *1912.*
        Provenance: the Bernheim-Jeune Gallery; the
        S. Shchukin collection; the Museum of Modern
        Western Art, Moscow, 1918.
        In the Hermitage since 1948. Inv. No. 8965

169   THE MOROCCAN AMIDO. Left panel of a triptych.
1912. Tangier
Oil on canvas. 146 × 62 cm
Signed below right: *Henri-Matisse*
The right panel, *The Mulatto Fatima*, is in the
M. Müller collection, Switzerland.
Provenance: the S. Shchukin collection; the Museum
of Modern Western Art, Moscow, 1918.
In the Hermitage since 1934. Inv. No. 7699

170   MOROCCAN WOMAN (ZORAH STANDING). Central
panel of a triptych. 1912. Tangier
Oil on canvas. 146 × 61 cm
The picture was exhibited at the Bernheim-Jeune
Gallery in April 1913 (No. 9) under the title *Zorah*.
Provenance: the S. Shchukin collection; the Museum
of Modern Western Art, Moscow, 1918; the Pushkin
Museum of Fine Arts, Moscow, 1948.
In the Hermitage since 1968. Inv. No. 10044

171 MOROCCAN IN GREEN. 1912—13. Tangier
Oil on canvas. 145 × 96.5 cm
On the back of the canvas is a paper sticker
with the inscription: *Mr. Henri Matisse.*
Hôtel de France. Tanger
The portrait depicts a Moroccan of the Riff tribe.
The picture was exhibited at the Bernheim-Jeune
Gallery in April 1913 (No. 5).
Provenance: the S. Shchukin collection; the Museum
of Modern Western Art, Moscow, 1918.
In the Hermitage since 1948. Inv. No. 9155

172   BOUQUET OF FLOWERS ON THE VERANDA.
1912—13. Tangier
Oil on canvas. 146 × 97 cm
The picture was exhibited at the Bernheim-Jeune
Gallery in April 1913 under the title *Arums* (No. 11).
Provenance: the S. Shchukin collection; the Museum
of Modern Western Art, Moscow, 1918.
In the Hermitage since 1934. Inv. No. 7700

175 YOUNG WOMAN IN A BLUE BLOUSE (PORTRAIT
OF LYDIA DELECTORSKAYA). 1939, September.
Rochefort-en-Yvelines
Oil on canvas. 35.4 × 27.3 cm
Signed below right: *À LYDIA H MATISSE oct 39*
Provenance: presented by the artist to
L. Delectorskaya, October 1, 1939; in the possession
of L. Delectorskaya, 1939.
In the Hermitage since 1971 (gift of L. Delectorskaya).
Inv. No. 10157

176 PORTRAIT OF LYDIA DELECTORSKAYA.
1947. Paris
Oil on canvas. 64.3 × 49.7 cm
Signed and dated below right: *H. Matisse 47.*
Provenance: in the possession of L. Delectorskaya,
1947.
In the Hermitage since 1967 (gift of L. Delectorskaya).
Inv. No. 10023

174 ARAB COFFEE-HOUSE. 1912—13. Tangier
Size colour on canvas. 176 × 210 cm

The picture was exhibited at the Bernheim-Jeune
Gallery in April 1913 (No. 2).

The Arabs were originally depicted in burnouses of
different colours (red, blue and yellow); there was
a row of shoes along the lower edge of the canvas.

Provenance: bought from the artist by S. Shchukin,
April 1913; the Museum of Modern Western Art,
Moscow, 1918.

In the Hermitage since 1948. Inv. No. 9661

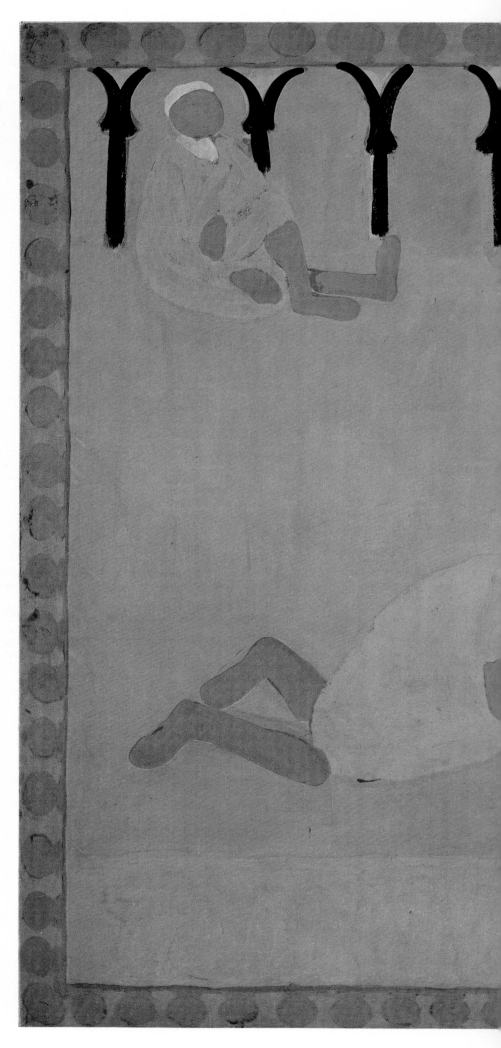

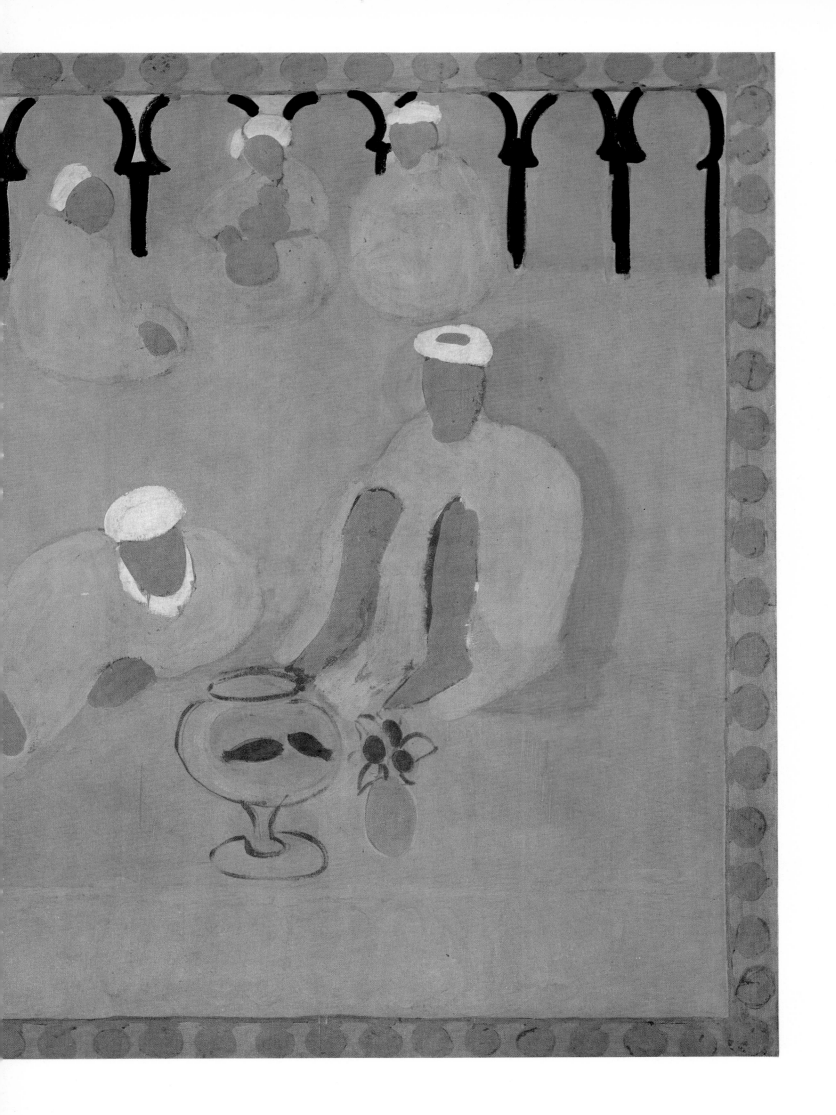

173   PORTRAIT OF THE ARTIST'S WIFE. 1912—13.
Issy-les-Moulineaux
Oil on canvas. 145 × 97 cm
Signed below right: *Henri Matisse*
The picture representing Amélie Matisse was
exhibited at the Salon d'Automne in 1913 (No. 1469).
Provenance: the S. Shchukin collection, 1914;
the Museum of Modern Western Art, Moscow, 1918.
In the Hermitage since 1948. Inv. No. 9156

OTHON FRIESZ
1879—1949

Othon Friesz, the son of a sea captain, was born in Le Havre. He studied at the lycée and attended, at the same time, the local school of fine arts where he was trained by Charles Lhuillier and made friends with Raoul Dufy.

When a young man of sixteen Friesz started painting landscapes of Normandy, which bore the stamp of Impressionism. In 1899 the town council of Le Havre granted him a scholarship to complete his artistic education in Paris. He enrolled at the Ecole Nationale des Beaux-Arts as a student of the academic painter Bonnat, but shortly afterwards left his studio. He first exhibited at the Salon des Indépendants in 1903. At the beginning of the 1900s Friesz broke with the Impressionist manner of painting *en plein air*. In 1905 he exhibited with the other Fauves at the Salon d'Automne. The works he produced in 1905 and 1906 at La Ciotat and Antwerp most clearly reflected his infatuation with Fauvism.

In 1907, however, his painterly manner radically changed: figures and objects in his canvases now assumed simplified, massive forms, and composition became dynamic.

In 1912 Friesz opened a school of painting in his studio, and subsequently taught at various academies in Paris. In 1914 he was called up and served in the Air Force. He returned to Paris in 1919.

In the 1920s—40s he remained faithful to his manner of 1908—14, painting mainly interiors, portraits, landscapes and still lifes. In 1937 he collaborated with Dufy in decorating the Palais Chaillot where he painted *The Seine*, a large mural.

177   ROOFS AND CATHEDRAL AT ROUEN. 1908
Oil on canvas. 119 × 95.5 cm
Signed and dated below right: *Othon Friesz 08*
The picture was exhibited at the Salon d'Automne in 1908 (No. 5717).
Provenance: the Druet Gallery; the S. Shchukin collection; the Museum of Modern Western Art, Moscow, 1918.
In the Hermitage since 1948. Inv. No. 9173

178 TEMPTATION (ADAM AND EVE). 1909
Oil on canvas. 73 × 60 cm
Signed below left: *Othon Friesz*
Sketch for the picture of the same name, exhibited
at the Salon des Indépendants in 1910 (No. 1969)
and at Friesz's one-man show at the Druet
Gallery in 1911
The edges of the painted canvas overlapping the
subframe suggest that the Hermitage sketch is
a clipping from a canvas of larger dimensions.
Provenance: the Druet Gallery; the I. Morozov
collection, 1911; the Museum of Modern Western
Art, Moscow, 1918.
In the Hermitage since 1948. Inv. No. 8960

179 A HILL. LANDSCAPE AT ANDELYS. 1908
Oil on canvas. 61 × 74 cm
Signed below right: *Othon Friesz*
The picture was exhibited at the Salon des
Indépendants in 1908 (No. 2357).
Provenance: the Druet Gallery; the I. Morozov
collection, 1908; the Museum of Modern Western Art,
Moscow, 1918.
In the Hermitage since 1930. Inv. No. 6543

180 STILL LIFE WITH A STATUETTE OF BUDDHA.
1909
Oil on canvas. 51 × 42 cm
The picture was exhibited at the Druet Gallery
in 1909 (No. 47).
Provenance: the Druet Gallery; bought by I. Morozov
through the agency of Mme Maurice Denis, 1909;
the Museum of Modern Western Art, Moscow, 1918.
In the Hermitage since 1930. Inv. No. 6544

181 TRAVAUX D'AUTOMNE. 1907
Oil on canvas. 54 × 65 cm
Signed in monogram below left: *OF*.
Sketch for the painting of the same name (1908,
National Gallery, Oslo)
The landscape background of the sketch is based
on the motifs of the artist's earlier canvas *Côte de
Grâce à Honfleur*.
The sketch was twice displayed in Moscow, at the
1909 Salon of the *Golden Fleece* magazine (No. 153)
and at the 1912 Exhibition of the Jack of Diamonds
group.
Provenance: the S. Shchukin collection; the Museum
of Modern Western Art, Moscow, 1918.
In the Hermitage since 1948. Inv. No. 8890

182   TULIPS AND DAISIES. 1910
Oil on canvas. 65 × 81 cm
Signed and dated in the left-hand corner:
Othon Friesz. 10

Provenance: the Druet Gallery; the I. Morozov
collection, 1910; the Museum of Modern Western Art,
Moscow, 1918.
In the Hermitage since 1934. Inv. No. 7727

HENRI LE FAUCONNIER
1881—1946

Henri Le Fauconnier, the son a doctor, was born and grew up at Hesdin (Pas-de-Calais). He came to Paris in 1900 to study law, but gave up the idea and entered the Académie Julian where he enrolled in the studio of Laurens. He began exhibiting at the Salon des Indépendants in 1904 and from 1907 onwards sent his works to the Salon d'Automne. His early work was close to Fauvism, but already in 1908, when the artist was active at Ploumanac'h (Brittany), his landscapes assumed new features foreshadowing the emerging Cubism. Shortly after that Le Fauconnier joined with Gleizes, Metzinger, Delaunay and made the acquaintance of Picasso. In 1911 he exhibited with other Cubist artists at the Salon des Indépendants and in 1912 his painting *Lake in the Mountains* was displayed at the show of the Jack of Diamonds group in Moscow. In that same year Le Fauconnier became head of the Académie de la Palette in Paris. He met young Munich artists, helped them in founding the Blaue Reiter group and contributed to their exhibitions. He also exhibited in Berlin, Prague, Budapest, Copenhagen, Zurich and Barcelona. In 1914 Le Fauconnier moved to Amsterdam where, together with several Dutch artists and writers, he founded the Signal group (1916) proclaiming a return to nature and a symbolic expressionism.

Le Fauconnier took part, together with Russian and Dutch artists, in the Signal group shows, but at the 1918 exhibition of French painters in The Hague his works were not accepted.

The period of 1918—19 saw the beginnings of a decline in his creative endeavour: this coincided with the severe mental illness of his wife. His long stay abroad resulted in the loss of his ties with almost all his friends in the artistic circles, and during many years after his return to Paris (1920) he lived in solitude, hardly ever taking up the brush.

Le Fauconnier died in his studio at the end of December 1945, but his body was not discovered until the beginning of the next year.

183   LITTLE SCHOOLGIRL. 1907

Oil on canvas. 73 × 92 cm

Signed and dated below right: *Le Fauconnier 07*

The picture was exhibited at the 1907 Salon d'Automne (No. 1061) and at the 1908 Salon of the *Golden Fleece* magazine in Moscow (No. 115).

Provenance: the D. Riabushinsky collection, Moscow; the Chetverikova collection, Moscow; the Museum of Modern Western Art, Moscow, 1940.

In the Hermitage since 1948. Inv. No. 8889

184 VILLAGE AMONG THE ROCKS (PLOUMANAC'H).
1910
Oil on canvas. 73 × 92 cm
Signed below right: *Le Fauconnier*
The picture was exhibited at the Salon d'Automne
in 1910 (No. 728).
Provenance: the S. Shchukin collection; the Museum
of Modern Western Art, Moscow, 1918.
In the Hermitage since 1948. Inv. No. 9181

185 LAKE IN THE MOUNTAINS. 1911
Oil on canvas. 91 × 72 cm
Signed below right: *Le Fauconnier*
The picture was exhibited at the Salon d'Automne
in 1911 (No. 877) under the title of *Village au bord
d'un lac* and at the show of the Jack of Diamonds
group in Moscow in 1912 (No. 211).
Provenance: bought by S. Poliakov at the Salon
d'Automne, 1911; the Tretyakov Gallery, 1919; the
Museum of Modern Western Art, Moscow, 1925.
In the Hermitage since 1948. Inv. No. 9170

186 THE SIGNAL. 1915
Oil on canvas. 80×99 cm
Provenance: the W. Beffie collection, Amsterdam;
donated by W. Beffie on the request
of Le Fauconnier to the Museum of Modern Western
Art, Moscow, 1934.
In the Hermitage since 1948. Inv. No. 9172

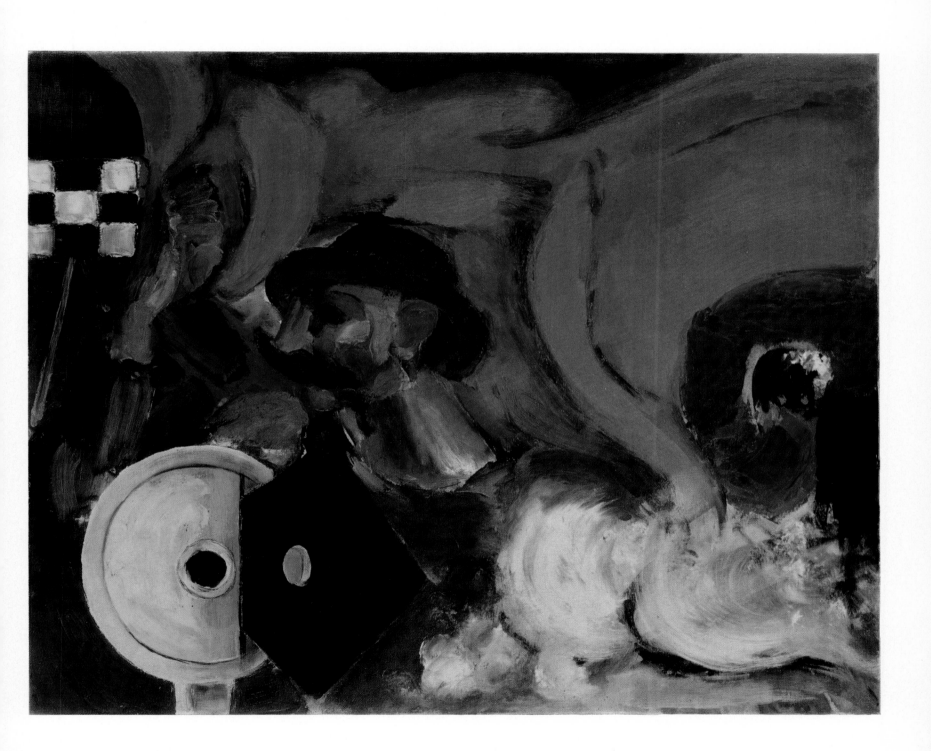

MAURICE DE VLAMINCK
1876—1958

Maurice de Vlaminck was born in Paris into the family of musicians. He mastered the technique of painting on his own, learned to play the violin and tried his hand at poetry and prose.

His friendship with Derain proved to be of great importance in his life. In 1900 both artists shared the same studio at Chatou, near Fournaise's restaurant where at the beginning of the 1880s Renoir painted his canvases. Through Derain Vlaminck made the acquaintance of Matisse and other Fauve artists. In 1905 and 1906 he first exhibited at the Salon d'Automne and the Salon des Indépendants.

The 1901 Van Gogh exhibition exerted a decisive influence on Vlaminck's artistic career: he found in the great Dutchman's work features akin to his own creative aspirations. Subsequently he drifted away from Van Gogh, having been greatly impressed by the Cézanne retrospective exhibition held in 1907. It was at this period that Vlaminck's paintings acquired new constructive elements.

During the First World War the artist painted sinister landscapes with an overcast sky, marked by an expressionism, the first signs of which had already been apparent in his early works.

In 1925 Vlaminck settled at Rueil-la-Gadelière (Eure-et-Loir), where he lived alone to his last days, continuing to produce landscapes and still lifes and writing articles.

187 VIEW OF THE SEINE. *C.* 1905—6
Oil on canvas. 54 × 64.5 cm
Signed below right: *Vlaminck*
Provenance: the Vollard collection; presented by A. Vollard to I. Morozov, 1908; the Museum of Modern Western Art, Moscow, 1918.
In the Hermitage since 1948. Inv. No. 9112

188   VIEW OF A SMALL TOWN. 1909
Oil on canvas. 73 × 92 cm
Signed below right: *Vlaminck*
Provenance: the Kahnweiler Gallery; the S. Shchukin
collection; the Museum of Modern Western Art,
Moscow, 1918.
In the Hermitage since 1930. Inv. No. 6539

189 VIEW OF A TOWN BY THE LAKE. *C.* 1907
Oil on canvas. 80 × 99 cm
Signed below left: *Vlaminck*
Provenance: the Kahnweiler Gallery; the S. Shchukin
collection; the Museum of Modern Western Art,
Moscow, 1918.
In the Hermitage since 1948. Inv. No. 9111

190 VIEW OF A SMALL TOWN WITH A CHURCH.
C. 1911
Oil on canvas. 72.5 × 91 cm
Signed below left: *Vlaminck*
Provenance: the Kahnweiler Gallery; the S. Shchukin
collection; the Museum of Modern Western Art,
Moscow, 1918.
In the Hermitage since 1948. Inv. No. 9113

191   HOUSE ON A HILL. 1920s
Oil on canvas. 33 × 41 cm
Signed below left: *Vlaminck*
In the Hermitage since 1972 (formerly in the
G. Sery collection). Inv. No. 10174

ANDRÉ DERAIN
1880—1954

André Derain was born in Chatou, near Paris. At the age of fifteen he set out to study painting on his own, sometimes acting on the advice of Jacomin who was an old friend of Cézanne. From 1898 to 1899 he attended the Académie Carrière, where he met Matisse and Puy. From 1900 onwards Derain shared a studio with his friend Vlaminck at Chatou. During this time he created his first drawings and woodcuts — illustrations for books by Vlaminck (1902—3), Apollinaire (1909), Jacob (1912), Breton (1916) and Reverdy (1921). He painted with Matisse at Collioure during the summer of 1905, mastering the technique of separate stroke, but in 1906 he moved away from Divisionism. In 1905 and 1906 he exhibited with other Fauve artists at the Salon d'Automne and the Salon des Indépendants. In 1907 Derain left Chatou and settled in Paris. There he made the acquaintance of the artists and poets of the Bateau-Lavoir group — Jacob, Apollinaire, Van Dongen, Braque and Picasso, travelling with the latter in Spain in 1910.

Derain used to spend his summers in the South of France: at Collioure (1905), at Cassy (1907), at Martigues (1908, 1909, 1913) and at Cagnes (1910)

After 1907 he developed a taste for Cubist structures, especially during his stay at Carrières-Saint-Denis where he worked with Braque in the summer of 1909, and also at Cagnes and Martigues. About the same time he was fascinated by Negro sculpture and naïve realism, and from 1913 to 1914, during his "Gothic" period, evinced an interest in the Sienese primitives and the Avignon school. In 1919 Derain designed décors and costumes for the Ballets Russes and in the 1930s for Balanchine's company in Monte Carlo. This later period was marked by a heightened attention to the traditions of seventeenth century art. Derain died in a car accident in 1954.

192   THE PORT AT LE HAVRE. *C.* 1905—6
Oil on canvas. 59 × 73 cm
Signed below right: *a derain*
Provenance: the Kahnweiler Gallery; the S. Shchukin
collection, 1914; the Museum of Modern Western Art,
Moscow, 1918.
In the Hermitage since 1930. Inv. No. 6540

193 ROAD IN THE MOUNTAINS. CASSIS. 1907
Oil on canvas. 80.5 × 99 cm
The picture was exhibited at the Salon des
Indépendants in 1908 (No. 6458).
Provenance: bought by I. Morozov at the Salon des
Indépendants, 1908; the Museum of Modern Western
Art, Moscow, 1918.
In the Hermitage since 1948. Inv. No. 9126

194 TABLE AND CHAIRS. *C.* 1912
Oil on canvas. 87 × 85.5 cm
Signed on the back: *a derain*
Provenance: the Kahnweiler Gallery; the I. Morozov
collection, 1913; the Museum of Modern Western Art,
Moscow, 1918.
In the Hermitage since 1948. Inv. No. 9127

195   STILL LIFE WITH SKULL. *C.* 1912
Oil on canvas. 72 × 119 cm
Signed on the back: *a derain*
Provenance: the Kahnweiler Gallery; the S. Shchukin
collection, 1912; the Museum of Modern Western Art,
Moscow, 1918.
In the Hermitage since 1948. Inv. No. 9084

196   LAKE. *C.* 1913—14
Oil on canvas. 99 × 65 cm
Signed on the back: *a derain*
Provenance: the Kahnweiler Gallery; the S. Shchukin
collection, 1914; the Museum of Modern Western Art,
Moscow, 1918.
In the Hermitage since 1934. Inv. No. 7719

197 THE GROVE. *C.* 1912
   Oil on canvas. 116 × 81 cm
   Signed on the back: *a derain*
   Provenance: the Kahnweiler Gallery; the S. Shchukin
   collection; the Museum of Modern Western Art,
   Moscow, 1918.
   In the Hermitage since 1948. Inv. No. 9085

198 MONTREUIL-SUR-MER (HARBOUR). 1910
   Oil on canvas. 60 × 102 cm
   Signed below right: *a derain*
   Provenance: the Kahnweiler Gallery; the S. Shchukin
   collection, 1914; the Museum of Modern Western Art,
   Moscow, 1918.
   In the Hermitage since 1934. Inv. No. 7720

199 EARTHENWARE JUG, WHITE SERVIETTE AND
FRUIT. *C.* 1912
Oil on canvas. 60 × 49 cm
Signed on the back: *a derain*
Provenance: the Kahnweiler Gallery; the S. Shchukin
collection; the Museum of Modern Western Art,
Moscow, 1918.
In the Hermitage since 1948. Inv. No. 8894

200 THE ROCKS AT VERS. 1912
Oil on canvas. 60 × 81 cm
Signed on the back: *a derain*
Provenance: the Kahnweiler Gallery; the S. Shchukin
collection; the Museum of Modern Western Art,
Moscow, 1918.
In the Hermitage since 1930. Inv. No. 6541

201 HARBOUR IN PROVENCE
(MARTIGUES). 1913
Oil on canvas. 140 × 89 cm
Signed on the back: *a derain*
Provenance: the Kahnweiler
Gallery; the S. Shchukin collection,
1914; the Museum of Modern Western
Art, Moscow, 1918.
In the Hermitage since 1948.
Inv. No. 9101

202   GIRL IN BLACK DRESS. Study. 1914
Oil on canvas. 93 × 60 cm
Signed on the back: *a derain*
Provenance: the Kahnweiler Gallery; the S. Shchukin
collection, 1914; the Museum of Modern Western Art,
Moscow, 1918.
In the Hermitage since 1931. Inv. No. 6577

203 STILL LIFE. *C*. 1912—13
Oil on canvas. 99 × 115 cm
Signed below right: *derain*
Provenance: the Kahnweiler Gallery; the S. Shchukin
collection; the Museum of Modern Western Art,
Moscow, 1918.
In the Hermitage since 1930. Inv. No. 6542

204 PORTRAIT OF A GIRL IN BLACK DRESS. 1914
Oil on canvas. 114.5 × 88 cm
Signed on the back: *a derain*
Provenance: the Kahnweiler Gallery; the S. Shchukin
collection, 1914; the Museum of Modern Western Art,
Moscow, 1918.
In the Hermitage since 1948. Inv. No. 9125

205   PORTRAIT OF AN UNKNOWN MAN WITH
      A NEWSPAPER ("CHEVALIER X"). 1914
      Oil on canvas. 160.5 × 96 cm
      Signed on the back: *a derain*
      Originally the newspaper was pasted on the picture.
      Provenance: the Kahnweiler Gallery; the S. Shchukin
      collection, 1914; the Museum of Modern Western
      Art, Moscow, 1918.
      In the Hermitage since 1948. Inv. No. 9128

KEES VAN DONGEN
1877—1968

Kees Van Dongen, a Dutchman by birth, was born and grew up at Delfshaven, a suburb of Rotterdam. From his early childhood he displayed a gift for painting. In 1892, at the age of fifteen, he began to study with J. Striening and J. Heiberg at the School of Fine Arts in Rotterdam. After finishing the school in 1897 Van Dongen settled in Paris and since then forever linked his destiny with France. During the first years of his stay in Paris Van Dongen lived in dire poverty and was compelled to take up any job that came his way: he worked as a house-painter and as a night porter at the Halles.

His artistic début at the Gallery of Le Barc de Boutteville evoked little response on the part of the public, nor did it improve his financial position. It was only in 1901 that Van Dongen managed to publish his drawings in the humour review *L'Assiette au Beurre* and then began contributing to the reviews *Le Rire*, *Gil Blas* and *Frou-Frou*; at the same time he continued to paint.

Towards the turn of the century the main tendency of Van Dongen's art was finally established. He derived his subject matter from the world of actors, dancers, singers and models. He preferred artificial light, painting in bright colours scenes at night cafés or cabarets. He participated with other Fauve artists in the Salon des Indépendants of 1906. In that same year Van Dongen was given his first one-man show at the Druet Gallery, which attracted the attention of both art collectors and dealers. In 1906 Kahnweiler signed an exclusive contract for the sale and exhibition of his works and two years later a similar contract was made with the Bernheim-Jeune Gallery. From then on Van Dongen enjoyed constant success. In 1906 he moved into the Bateau-Lavoir in Montmartre where his neighbours were Picasso and Juan Gris and where he regularly met Max Jacob, Apollinaire and Mac Orlan. Between 1910 and 1911 Van Dongen visited Spain and Morocco. In 1912 he taught painting at the Académie Vitti. By this time his one-man shows had been held in Berlin, Munich, Brussels and London.

At the end of the First World War Van Dongen had already become one of the most fashionable artists in Europe. He was the painter in demand: kings and ministers, famous actresses and aristocrats all wanted their portraits painted by Van Dongen. Many of his works of this period are executed in a superficial way. However, the best of his portraits retained Van Dongen's manner and a light irony in the treatment of characters.

In the 1920s the artist's fame reached its height. His one-man shows followed one another. In 1926 he was made Chevalier of the Légion d'Honneur. But it was only in 1929 that he was granted French citizenship.

From 1957 Van Dongen lived in Monaco. He died in Monte Carlo.

206   SPRING. *C.* 1908
Oil on canvas. 80 × 99 cm
Signed below right: *Van Dongen*
The picture was exhibited at the Bernheim-Jeune
Gallery in 1908 under the title *Le Printemps* (No. 47).
Provenance: the Bernheim-Jeune Gallery; the
S. Shchukin collection; the Museum of Modern
Western Art, Moscow, 1918.
In the Hermitage since 1948. Inv. No. 9130

207   DANCER IN RED. 1907
      Oil on canvas. 99 × 80 cm
      Signed below left: *Van Dongen*.
      The picture was exhibited in Moscow at the Salon
      of the *Golden Fleece* magazine in 1909 (No. 34).
      Provenance: the N. Riabushinsky collection, Moscow;
      the M. Mazurin collection, Moscow; the Sixth
      Proletarian Museum, Moscow, 1918; the Museum of
      Modern Western Art, Moscow, 1920.
      In the Hermitage since 1948. Inv. No. 9129

208 WOMAN IN A BLACK HAT. *C.* 1908
Oil on canvas. 100 × 81 cm
Signed below right: *Van Dongen*

Provenance: the Kahnweiler Gallery; the S. Shchukin
collection; the Museum of Modern Western Art,
Moscow, 1918.
In the Hermitage since 1931. Inv. No. 6572

209   ANTONIA LA COQUINERA
Oil on canvas. 93 × 80 cm
Signed below left: *Van Dongen*
Provenance: the Kahnweiler Gallery; the S. Shchukin
collection; the Museum of Modern Western Art,
Moscow, 1918.
In the Hermitage since 1948. Inv. No. 8994

210   LUCIE AND HER PARTNER. 1911

Oil on canvas. 130 × 90 cm

Signed below left: *Van Dongen*

The date and title of the picture are given on the evidence of the Bernheim-Jeune Gallery's label on the back of the canvas.

Provenance: the Bernheim-Jeune Gallery; the M. Zetlin collection, Moscow; the Poryvkina collection, Moscow; the Museum of Modern Western Art, Moscow, 1939.

In the Hermitage since 1948. Inv. No. 9087

GEORGES ROUAULT
1871—1958

Georges Rouault, the son of a cabinet maker, was born and lived all his life in Paris. At fourteen he was apprenticed to Hirsch, a stained-glass painter, and worked on the restoration of medieval windows. Several years of mastering this craft developed in him a taste for large iridescent coloured planes encircled with a vigorous black line, a taste which to a certain extent was conducive in shaping his painterly manner. During his apprenticeship Rouault attended evening courses at the Ecole des Arts Décoratifs. In 1891 he entered the Ecole Nationale des Beaux-Arts where his teachers were Delaunay and later Gustave Moreau. He became a close friend of Moreau and in 1898, after his teacher's death, was appointed Keeper of the Musée Gustave Moreau.

When studying with Moreau, Rouault painted compositions on religious themes. One of them, *Christ among the Teachers* (1894), was awarded the Prix Chenavard. The peculiarity of Rouault's artistic manner was first reflected in his sombre, dramatic landscapes done in the late 1890s and already free from academic influence. But it was only in 1904—5 that his works exhibited at the Salon d'Automne revealed the features which were to distinguish his subsequent works: the tragic interpretation of images, the generalized manner of painting, black contours and luminous colours. His gallery of judges, strolling ac-robats and prostitutes produced in the 1910s demonstrates all these characteristics. Rouault painted in oils, water-colours and gouaches, and devoted much time to ceramics.

His art developed apart from the two major movements of the time, Fauvism and Cubism, though he constantly associated with Matisse and other painters of his circle. His searchings had much in common with the aspirations of German Expressionists.

In 1917 Rouault undertook an extensive series of etchings to illustrate *Les Réincarnations du Père Ubu*, *Le Cirque de l'Etoile Filante*, *Les Passions*, and *Les Fleurs du Mal* of Baudelaire; for many years he did engravings for the suite *Miserere et Guerre*, its title derived from the first words of the 51st Psalm. Though finished in 1927, the suite was published by Vollard only in 1948. These plates are executed in a strictly individual and novel technique and are accompanied by captions of a highly expressive and imaginative character.

In 1928 he created the settings and costumes for Diaghilev's production of *Le Fils prodigue* to the music by Prokofiev.

From 1932 onwards the artist concentrated his attention on oil paintings. During his last ten years Rouault painted, beside landscapes, numerous compositions with clowns and pierrots.

211   FILLES. 1907
Pastel and tempera on paper. 97 × 65 cm
Signed and dated above right: *G. Rouault. 907.*
Dated again below: *1907*
The picture was exhibited at the 1908 Salon of the *Golden Fleece* magazine in Moscow (No. 150).
Provenance: the Druet Gallery; the N. Riabushinsky collection, Moscow, 1908; the V. Nosov collection, Moscow; the First Proletarian Museum, Moscow, 1918; the Museum of Modern Western Art, Moscow, 1923. In the Hermitage since 1948. Inv. No. 43783

212   SPRING. 1911

Water-colour and pastel on paper. 55 × 52 cm (oval)
Signed and dated below right: *1911 G. Rouault*

The picture was exhibited at the Salon des
Indépendants in 1911 (No. 5278) under the title
Paysage (Printemps).

Provenance: bought by I. Morozov at the Salon des
Indépendants through the agency of Druet, 1911; the
Museum of Modern Western Art, Moscow, 1918.
In the Hermitage since 1934. Inv. No. 42157

MARIE LAURENCIN
1885—1956

Marie Laurencin was born in Paris. After graduating from the Lycée Lamartine where she had a rather poor record, Laurencin was attracted to poetry and subsequently published her verse under the pen-name of Louise Lalanne. She attended evening drawing classes at the School of Art in Sèvres. Later on she studied painting at the Académie Humbert. From 1905 onwards she moved in the Cubist milieu of the Bateau-Lavoir group. Though she constantly took part in the discussions of the future Cubists, her subtle and lyrical art was hardly influenced either by Picasso or any other members of the Bateau-Lavoir group.

Laurencin painted in oils, mostly portraits and fantastic scenes. She also did drawings and water-colours. She illustrated *La Tentative amoureuse* by André Gide, *Les Brontë, filles du vent* by René Crevel, and Lewis Carroll's *Alice in Wonderland*.

In 1924 Laurencin designed the décor of *Les Biches* by Francis Poulenc for Diaghilev's Russian ballet. In the 1920s portraiture began to occupy a dominant place in her work. However, in her incessant production of portraits Marie Laurencin eventually lost the individual style characteristic of the peak of her artistic career.

213 BACCHANTE. 1911
     Oil on cardboard. 32.5 × 41 cm
     Signed below right: *Marie Laurencin*
     Provenance: the S. Shchukin collection; the Museum
     of Modern Western Art, Moscow, 1918.
     In the Hermitage since 1948. Inv. No. 9069

214 ARTEMIS. *C.* 1908
     Oil on canvas pasted on cardboard. 35 × 27 cm
     Signed below right: *Laurencin.*
     Provenance: the S. Shchukin collection; the Museum
     of Modern Western Art, Moscow, 1918.
     In the Hermitage since 1948. Inv. No. 9000

PABLO PICASSO
1881—1973

Pablo Picasso, a Spaniard by birth, was born in Málaga and was first trained by his father, José Ruiz Blasco, a professor of drawing at the School of Arts and Crafts in Málaga (from 1895 he taught in Barcelona). At sixteen Picasso entered the San-Fernando Academy in Madrid. In 1897 his *Knowledge and Mercy*, painted in the style of classical art, won him a gold medal at an exhibition in Málaga. However, the young artist was not satisfied with his academic successes. In 1899 he joined up with the circle of Barcelona artists and poets who met at the cabaret "The Four Cats" and took part in their exhibition. In October of the same year he first came to Paris, where he finally settled in 1904. He established himself in Montmartre, in the Bateau-Lavoir, 13 rue Ravignan, a house inhabited by young artists and writers. It was here, in an atmosphere of friendly contact and lively discussions with Apollinaire, Matisse, Derain, Jacob and Braque, that the artistic idiom of the young Picasso took shape. His "Blue" period (1901—4, Barcelona and Paris) was followed by the "Rose" period (1905—6, Montmartre) with its recurrent theme of acrobats and harlequins. Then he embarked on a new quest, turning to the art of the primitive peoples of Africa (the "Negro" period, 1907—8), evolved a new concept of space and form (Analytical Cubism, 1909—11) and elaborated the prin-

ciples of Synthetic Cubism (1912—14). In the décor and designs for Diaghilev's ballet *Parade* (1917) he evinced an interest in the interrelationship of planar and spatial elements. His "Neo-Classical" period lasted from 1921 to 1924; to this time belong, besides his Cubist canvases, several works influenced by the painting of Ingres. Between 1925 and 1935 Picasso was attracted by the problems that were also being tackled by the Surrealists. During these years he worked on sculpture, drawings, paintings, and wrote poetry. In 1937 he created his monumental composition *Guernica*, a great memorial to the time of struggle against Fascism.

During the Second World War Picasso lived in Paris, aiding the French Resistance movement. In 1944 he joined the French Communist Party. From 1948 on he took an active part in various Peace Congresses throughout Europe. In the 1950s Picasso divided his time between Antibes and Vallauris; he worked at decorative ceramics, painted the large canvases *War* and *Peace*, and produced a number of graphic and sculptural pieces.

In 1961 Picasso moved to his estate in Mougins (Alpes Maritimes) and lived there till his last days.

In 1963 the Pablo Picasso Museum was inaugurated in Barcelona. To this city, where his artistic career had begun, Picasso donated 994 of his works.

215 WOMAN DRINKING ABSINTH. 1901. Paris
Oil on canvas. 73 × 59 cm
Signed above right: -*Picasso*
This picture is sometimes called *L'Apéritif*.
Provenance: the Kahnweiler Gallery; the S. Shchukin collection, 1911; the Museum of Modern Western Art, Moscow, 1918.
In the Hermitage since 1948. Inv. No. 9045

216

THE VISIT (TWO SISTERS).
1902. Barcelona
Oil on canvas pasted on a
panel. 152 × 100 cm
Signed and dated above right:
Picasso 1902

The preliminary sketches for
the picture were made at the
Saint-Lazare Hospital in Paris.
One of the sketches, depicting
the sick woman and the nun,
bears the inscription: *Les
deux sœurs.*
Provenance: the S. Shchukin
collection; the Museum of
Modern Western Art,
Moscow, 1918.
In the Hermitage since 1948.
Inv. No. 9071

217   PORTRAIT OF A YOUNG WOMAN.
       1903. Barcelona
       Oil on canvas pasted on cardboard. 50 × 36 cm
       The infra-red examination shows the author's
       inscription in the top left-hand corner: *à Henri*
       Bloch Picasso
       Provenance: the S. Shchukin collection; the Museum
       of Modern Western Art, Moscow, 1918.
       In the Hermitage since 1931. Inv. No. 6573

218   PORTRAIT OF SOLER. 1903, summer. Barcelona
       Oil on canvas. 100 × 70 cm
       Signed and dated above left: *Picasso 1903*
       José María Soler, a fashionable Barcelona tailor,
       was Picasso's friend and a patron of young artists.
       Provenance: the Soler collection, Barcelona; the
       Kahnweiler Gallery; the S. Shchukin collection;
       the Museum of Modern Western Art, Moscow, 1918.
       In the Hermitage since 1930. Inv. No. 6528

219   MALE FIGURE AND A MAN'S HEAD IN PROFILE
Sketches on the back of the picture *Boy with a Dog*
Oil on cardboard. 57.2 × 41.2 cm
See No. 220.

220   BOY WITH A DOG. 1905. Paris
Pastel and gouache on cardboard. 57.2 × 41.2 cm
Signed above left: *Picasso 05*
This picture belongs to the series of works related
to the large composition *Family of Saltimbanques.*
Provenance: the S. Shchukin collection; the Museum
of Modern Western Art, Moscow, 1918.
In the Hermitage since 1931. Inv. No. 41158

221 NAKED YOUTH. 1906, spring. Paris
Sepia and tempera on cardboard. 66.2 × 50 cm
Signed below right: *Picasso*
On the back is a charcoal drawing representing
a boy seated and a woman lying.
This is one of the studies for the canvases
Bathing a Horse and *Boy Leading a Horse*
which remained unfinished.
Provenance: the S. Shchukin collection; the Museum
of Modern Western Art, Moscow, 1918.
In the Hermitage since 1934. Inv. No. 40777

222 GLASS VESSELS. 1906, summer.
Gosol (the Pyrenees)
Oil on canvas. 38.4 × 56 cm
Signed below right: *Picasso*
Provenance: the Kahnweiler Gallery; the S. Shchukin
collection; the Museum of Modern Western Art,
Moscow, 1918.
In the Hermitage since 1948. Inv. No. 8895

223   NUDE (half-length). 1907
      Oil on canvas. 61 × 47 cm
      This is one of the works related to the composition
      Les Demoiselles d'Avignon.
      Provenance: the Vollard collection (judging by the
      inscription *Vollard* made in chalk on the back of the
      canvas); the S. Shchukin collection; the Museum of
      Modern Western Art, Moscow, 1918.
      In the Hermitage since 1948. Inv. No. 9046

224   THE DANCE OF THE VEILS. 1907, summer. Paris
      Oil on canvas. 150 × 100 cm
      Signed on the back, on the subframe: *Picasso*
      Provenance: the Leo and Gertrude Stein collection,
      Paris; the Vollard collection; the S. Shchukin
      collection; the Museum of Modern Western Art,
      Moscow, 1918.
      In the Hermitage since 1948. Inv. No. 9089

225 COMPOSITION WITH A SKULL.
1907, autumn. Paris
Oil on canvas. 115 × 88 cm
Signed on the back: *Picasso*

Provenance: the Kahnweiler Gallery; the S. Shchukin
collection, 1912; the Museum of Modern Western Art,
Moscow, 1918.
In the Hermitage since 1948. Inv. No. 9162

226 LA BAIGNADE
Oil on canvas. 38 × 62.5 cm
Signed on the back: *Picasso*
Provenance: the Kahnweiler Gallery;
the S. Shchukin collection; the Museum
of Modern Western Art,
Moscow, 1918.
In the Hermitage since 1948.
Inv. No. 8896

227 DRYAD. 1908
Oil on canvas. 185 × 108 cm
Signed on the back: *Picasso*
Provenance: the Kahnweiler Gallery; the S. Shchukin
collection; the Museum of Modern Western Art,
Moscow, 1918.
In the Hermitage since 1934. Inv. No. 7704

228 WOMAN SEATED. 1908
Oil on canvas. 150 × 99 cm
Signed on the back: *Picasso*
Provenance: the Kahnweiler Gallery; the S. Shchukin
collection; the Museum of Modern Western Art,
Moscow, 1918.
In the Hermitage since 1948. Inv. No. 9163

229 FRIENDSHIP. 1908
     Oil on canvas. 152 × 101 cm
     Signed on the back: *Picasso*
     Provenance: the Kahnweiler Gallery; the S. Shchukin
     collection; the Museum of Modern Western Art,
     Moscow, 1918.
     In the Hermitage since 1931. Inv. No. 6576

230   LA FERMIÈRE (half-length). 1908, summer.
Rue-des-Bois
Oil on canvas. 81 × 65 cm
Signed on the back: *Picasso*
The model was Picasso's landlady, Mme Putman.
Provenance: the Kahnweiler Gallery; the S. Shchukin
collection; the Museum of Modern Western Art,
Moscow, 1918.
In the Hermitage since 1930. Inv. No. 6531

231   LA FERMIÈRE (full-length). 1908, summer.
Rue-des-Bois
Oil on canvas. 81 × 56 cm
Signed on the back: *Picasso*
The same model as in No. 230.
Provenance: the Kahnweiler Gallery; the S. Shchukin
collection; the Museum of Modern Western Art,
Moscow, 1918.
In the Hermitage since 1948. Inv. No. 9161

232   WOMAN WITH A FAN (AFTER THE BALL). 1908,
summer. Paris
Oil on canvas. 150 × 100 cm
Provenance: the S. Shchukin collection; the Museum
of Modern Western Art, Moscow, 1918.
In the Hermitage since 1934. Inv. No. 7705

233 GREEN BOWL AND BLACK BOTTLE. 1908
Oil on canvas. 61 × 51 cm
Signed on the back: *Picasso*
The picture was exhibited at the Grafton Calleries
in London in 1912 (No. 60) as the property
of Leo Stein.
Provenance: the Leo Stein collection, Paris; the
Kahnweiler Gallery; the S. Shchukin collection, 1914;
the Museum of Modern Western Art, Moscow, 1918.
In the Hermitage since 1934. Inv. No. 7702

234   POT, WINE-GLASS AND BOOK. 1908
Oil on canvas. 55 × 46 cm
Provenance: the S. Shchukin collection; the Museum
of Modern Western Art, Moscow, 1918.
In the Hermitage since 1930. Inv. No. 6532

235 DECANTER AND TUREENS. 1908
Oil on cardboard. 66 × 50.5 cm
Signed on the back: *Picasso*
As a recent X-ray photograph shows, the picture
was painted over an earlier landscape dated 1901.
Provenance: the Kahnweiler Gallery; the S. Shchukin
collection; the Museum of Modern Western Art,
Moscow, 1918.
In the Hermitage since 1948. Inv. No. 8986

236 HOUSE IN A GARDEN. 1908, summer. Rue-des-Bois
Oil on canvas. 73 × 61 cm
Signed on the back: *Picasso*
Provenance: the Kahnweiler Gallery; the S. Shchukin
collection; the Museum of Modern Western Art,
Moscow, 1918.
In the Hermitage since 1930. Inv. No. 6535

237 THREE WOMEN. 1908. Paris
Oil on canvas. 200 × 185 cm
Signed on the back: *Picasso*
Provenance: the Leo and Gertrude Stein collection,
Paris; the Kahnweiler Gallery; the S. Shchukin
collection; the Museum of Modern Western Art,
Moscow, 1918.
In the Hermitage since 1948. Inv. No. 9658

238　FLOWERS IN A GREY JUG AND WINE-GLASS
WITH SPOON. 1908, summer. Rue-des-Bois
Oil on canvas. 81 × 65 cm
Signed on the back: *Picasso*
Provenance: the Kahnweiler Gallery; the S. Shchukin
collection; the Museum of Modern Western Art,
Moscow, 1918.
In the Hermitage since 1948. Inv. No. 8999

239   WOMAN PLAYING THE MANDOLIN. 1909. Paris
Oil on canvas. 91 × 72.5 cm
The picture was displayed at the International
Impressionist Exhibition in the House of Art,
Budapest, 1910 (No. 13), as the property of M. Nemes.
Provenance: the M. Nemes collection, Budapest;
the Kahnweiler Gallery; the S. Shchukin collection,
1914; the Museum of Modern Western Art,
Moscow, 1918.
In the Hermitage since 1931. Inv. No. 6579

240   MAN WITH ARMS CROSSED. 1909
      Water-colour, gouache and charcoal on paper
      pasted on cardboard. 65.5 × 49.5 cm
      Signed on the back: *Picasso*

      Provenance: the Kahnweiler Gallery; the S. Shchukin
      collection; the Museum of Modern Western Art,
      Moscow, 1918.
      In the Hermitage since 1948. Inv. No. 43481

241   FEMALE NUDE. 1909
      Oil on canvas. 100 × 81 cm
      Signed on the back: *Picasso*

      Provenance: the S. Shchukin collection; the Museum
      of Modern Western Art, Moscow, 1918.
      In the Hermitage since 1934. Inv. No. 7701

242   BOWL WITH FRUIT (STILL LIFE WITH A BOWL
OF FRUIT). 1909, spring. Paris
Oil on canvas. 92 × 72.5 cm
Signed on the back: *Picasso*
Provenance: the Kahnweiler Gallery; the S. Shchukin
collection; the Museum of Modern Western Art,
Moscow, 1918.
In the Hermitage since 1948. Inv. No. 9160

243   YOUNG LADY. 1909
Oil on canvas. 91 × 72.5 cm
Signed on the back: *Picasso*
Provenance: the Kahnweiler Gallery; the S. Shchukin
collection; the Museum of Modern Western Art,
Moscow, 1918.
In the Hermitage since 1948. Inv. No. 9159

244   FACTORY IN HORTA DE EBRO. 1909, summer.
Horta de Ebro
Oil on canvas. 53 × 60 cm
Provenance: the S. Shchukin collection; the Museum
of Modern Western Art, Moscow, 1918.
In the Hermitage since 1948. Inv. No. 9047

245   BOTTLE OF PERNOD (TABLE IN A CAFÉ).
1912, spring
Oil on canvas. 45.5 $\times$ 32.5 cm
Signed on the back: *Picasso*

Provenance: the Kahnweiler Gallery; the S. Shchukin
collection, 1912; the Museum of Modern Western Art,
Moscow, 1918.
In the Hermitage since 1948. Inv. No. 8920

246   VIOLIN AND GUITAR. 1913
Oil on canvas. 65 × 54 cm
Signed on the back: *Picasso*
Provenance: the Kahnweiler Gallery; the S. Shchukin
collection; the Museum of Modern Western Art,
Moscow, 1918.
In the Hermitage since 1948. Inv. No. 9048

247   MUSICAL INSTRUMENTS. 1912, summer. Sorgues
Oil, sawdust and gypsum on cardboard.
98 × 80 cm (oval)
Provenance: the Kahnweiler Gallery; the S. Shchukin
collection; the Museum of Modern Western Art,
Moscow, 1918.
In the Hermitage since 1948. Inv. No. 8939

248   CLARINET AND VIOLIN. 1913, spring
Oil on canvas. 55 × 33 cm
Signed in monogram below right: *P*
Signed on the back: *Picasso*
Provenance: the Kahnweiler Gallery; the S. Shchukin
collection; the Museum of Modern Western Art,
Moscow, 1918.
In the Hermitage since 1930. Inv. No. 6530

249   COMPOSITION. BOWL OF FRUIT AND SLICED
PEAR. 1914, April
Wallpaper, gouache and plumbago on cardboard.
35 × 32 cm
Signed and dated above right: *Picasso 4/1914.*
Provenance: the Kahnweiler Gallery; the S. Shchukin
collection; the Museum of Modern Western Art,
Moscow, 1918.
In the Hermitage since 1934. Inv. No. 42159

251 TAVERH (THE HAM). 1912
Oil and sawdust on cardboard. 29,5×38 cm (oval)
Provenance: the Kahnweiler Gallery; the S. Shchukin
collection; the Museum of Modern Western Art,
Moscow, 1918.
In the Hermitage since 1948, Inv. No. 8936

250   FRUIT VASE AND BUNCH OF GRAPES.
1914, spring

Paper, gouache, tempera, sawdust and pencil.
68 × 53 cm
Signed below right: *Picasso*

Provenance: the Kahnweiler Gallery; the S. Shchukin
collection; the Museum of Modern Western Art,
Moscow, 1918.
In the Hermitage since 1948. Inv. No. 43758

ANDRÉ LHOTE
1885—1962

André Lhote was born in Bordeaux. Complying with his father's wish, he began to train as a wood-carver, then worked in an atelier of decorative sculpture. At the same time he studied at the local school of fine arts. His earliest works were influenced by Gauguin's painting.

He first exhibited at the Salon d'Automne in 1907 and later at the Salon des Indépendants. During these years his art underwent a transformation: he became fascinated with Cézanne and turned to constructive painting. In 1911, in his quest for structured compositions, he made contact with the Cubists.

During the First World War Lhote lived in Arcachon, where he joined with the young artists and poets, Cocteau, Severini, Lipchitz and Rivera. On returning to Paris in 1917 he elaborated the principles of Synthetic Cubism (panel *Rugby*). He shared his ideas with his pupils at various Paris Academies, where he taught between 1918 and 1926. He published numerous books on the theory of painting, among them *Traité du paysage*, *Traité de la figure* and *Ecrits sur l'art*. Lhote painted several vast decorative compositions: the panels *Gas* for the Palais de la Découverte in Paris (1937) and *Glory to Bordeaux* for the University of Bordeaux (1955). He also did cartoons for tapestries.

In 1955 Lhote was elected President of the International Association of Artists, his candidacy being proposed by UNESCO. In 1958 he was made Commander of the Order of the Arts and Literature.

252   GREEN LANDSCAPE
Oil on canvas. 55 × 46 cm
Signed below left: *A. Lhote*
Provenance: the L. Zborowski collection, Paris; donated by L. Zborowski to the Museum of Modern Western Art, Moscow, 1927.
In the Hermitage since 1948. Inv. No. 8914

AMÉDÉE OZENFANT
1886—1966

Amédée Ozenfant was born in Saint-Quentin, France, and educated in Spain. Later, in his native town, he attended the local school of drawing and copied the pastels of La Tour, before going to Paris to study at the Académie de la Palette under Cottet and Jacques-Emile Blanche. Between 1915 and 1917 Ozenfant laid down the principles of Purism in art, which he propagated in his magazine *L'Elan*. In 1917 he met Charles-Edouard Jeanneret, who later became known as Le Corbusier; together they published *Après le Cubisme* (1919), a manifesto of Purism. From 1921 to 1925 Ozenfant and Jeanneret published their magazine *L'Esprit Nouveau*, advancing in it the idea of a synthesis of all forms of art. Many famous artists and writers including Aragon, Eluard, Cocteau, Ehrenburg, Cendrars and Carrà contributed to this magazine. In 1928 Ozenfant published an extensive work on modern art which has been reprinted many times in several languages (*Art*: I. *Bilan des arts modernes*; II. *Structure d'un nouvel esprit*) and developed the theory of monumental painting. During the same years he created two large mural compositions, *The Four Races* (1925—28) and *Life* (1931—38), now housed in the Museum of Modern Art in Paris. From 1935 to 1938 Ozenfant lived mainly in London, where he opened a school of modern painting. In 1938 he went to New York and there founded the Ozenfant School of Fine Arts.

In 1955 Ozenfant returned to France and settled at Cannes. During his late period he painted mainly the sea and ships, retaining the strict geometry of form and pictorial clarity characteristic of his œuvre.

253 STILL LIFE WITH BOTTLES. 1920
Oil on canvas. 80 × 62 cm
Signed and dated below right: *Ozenfant mil neuf cent vingt*
The picture was bought from the artist by the Museum of Modern Western Art, Moscow, in 1925. In the Hermitage since 1948. Inv. No. 9070

FERNAND LÉGER
1811—1955

Fernand Léger, the son of a farmer, was born in Argentan, Normandy. He attended the local lycée and in 1897 became an apprentice in an architect's office in Caen. Later, having moved to Paris, he studied at the Ecole des Arts Décoratifs under the sculptor Gérome and at the Ecole des Beaux-Arts under the painter Ferrier.

During his early period Léger fell under the influence of Impressionism. However, the 1907 Cézanne retrospective exhibition strongly affected his artistic outlook. By 1910 he had developed a Cubist style of his own. About the same time he joined the young artists Delaunay, Le Fauconnier, Gleizes, Picabia and Kupka when they met at Jacques Villon's, which led to the founding of the Salon de la Section d'Or. In 1911 Léger exhibited his Cubist *Nudes in a Forest* at the Salon des Indépendants.

At the outbreak of the First World War he was called up and fought at the front. Those years saw the beginnings of the new tendencies in the artist's work, engendered by his fascination with geometric figures and machine forms. By 1920, however, human figures began to reappear in his compositions (*The Mechanic*, *Women in an Interior*, etc.).

From 1924 onwards, during his "static" period, the dynamic shapes of machinery yielded place in the artist's works to calm planar forms (*Mural Paintings* series). In conjunction with the Purists, Ozenfant and Le Corbusier, Léger was busy working out a theory of the synthesis of architecture and painting. In 1925 he painted his first murals for the Pavillon de l'Esprit Nouveau built to Le Corbusier's design at the World Exhibition of Decorative Arts in Paris.

In the 1920s and 1930s the artist plunged into a very intense and highly versatile activity. In addition to oil paintings, he designed the décors and costumes for the ballets *Skating Rink* and *Création du Monde* by Milhaud, and *The Birth of the City* by Milhaud and Honegger; he was co-producer of several films and created his own film, *Le Ballet Mécanique.*

In the mid-1930s Léger joined the Association of Revolutionary Writers and Artists and supervised the decoration of mass spectacles, paricularly the Trade-Union festival organized by the World Confederation of Labour at the Vélodrome d'Hiver in Paris (1937). He also worked on the large-size panels *Adam and Eve*, *Composition with Two Parrots*, and others (in his own words, "peinture de grands sujets").

During the Second World War Léger lived in New York. He kept tackling the "grands sujets", among which were *The Swimmers* and *The Acrobats* series, *The Dance* and *The Three Musicians*. It was at this period that the artist experimented with a new device of introducing into his compositions transparent colour planes with a distinct outline showing through. This device was to become an indispensable element of his later works.

On his return to France in 1945 Léger joined the Communist Party. He took part in the Peace Congresses in Wroclaw and Vienna. Continuing to work on the large-size paintings, *The Builders*, *Leisure*, *Walk in the Countryside* and *July 14*, he produced, at the same time, a number of monumental and decorative pieces: mosaics, stained-glass windows, ceramics and cartoons for tapestries. He also tried his hand at sculpture and lithography.

In 1960 Léger's pupils made a huge mosaic panel after a 1952 design by the artist. This panel of 450 square metres now decorates the façade of the Musée Fernand Léger opened in Biot.

254   COMPOSITION. 1924
Oil on canvas. 73 × 92 cm
Signed and dated below right: *F. LÉGER.—24*
The picture was donated to the Museum of Modern
Western Art, Moscow, by B. Ternovets in 1927.
In the Hermitage since 1948. Inv. No. 9146

255 CARTE POSTALE
Oil on canvas. 92 × 65 cm.
Signed below right: *F. LÉGER.*
The picture was presented to the Soviet Union
by a group of Léger's pupils in 1949.
In the Hermitage since 1953. Inv. No. 9726

LÉOPOLD SURVAGE
1879—1968

Leopoldij Sturzwasgh (known as Survage), the son of a Moscow piano manufacturer of Finnish origin, received his artistic training at the Moscow School of Painting, Sculpture and Architecture where his teachers were L. Pasternak and K. Korovin.

In July 1908 Survage moved to Paris and there studied for a brief time at the art school of Matisse. For the next seven years he painted only in his spare time, earning his living as a piano tuner at the Salle Pleyel.

He joined the Cubists at their Salon d'Automne exhibition in 1911. In 1912—13 he produced an extensive series of *Rythmes colorés*, which to a certain extent foreshadowed the emergence of kinetic art.

Survage's work may be divided into several stages: his "rose" period of 1914—19 was superseded by the period of "muted tones" when he resorted to rigorously constructed composition and based his colour scale on an interplay of browns and greys.

In 1919 Survage became secretary of the Section d'Or, an international association of writers and artists including Gleizes, Braque, Arkhipenko, Marcoussis and Férat. The Section d'Or organized exhibitions in many large cities of Western Europe; among the participants were Léger, Villon, Goncharova, Larionov, Van Doesburg, Mondrian and Prampolini.

The year 1922 marked the emergence of the new, "back-to-Classicism" period in Survage's artistic development, a period when the portrayal of man became dominant in his works. It was at this time that Survage designed the costumes and décors for Diaghilev's production of Stravinsky's ballet *Mavra*.

During his Collioure period (1927—32) and the so-called "Synthetic" period the artist painted his most important canvases: *Oxman, Baigneuses, Escape of the Bull, Adam and Eve, The Golden Age* and *The Fall of Icarus*.

In 1937 Survage painted murals for the Pavillon de l'Union des Artistes Modernes at the Paris International Exhibition (jointly with Léger and Gleizes), for the Palais des Chemins de Fer and for the hall of the Salon de l'Aviation. His novel technique, which demanded the use of casein emulsions, proved especially successful while he decorated the International Palace of Congresses in Liège (1958). He also did cartoons for Gobelin (1957) and Aubusson tapestries (1961). Between 1951 and 1964 Survage worked on a large series of line drawings.

256   LANDSCAPE. 1925
Oil on canvas. 54 × 73 cm
Signed and dated below right: *Survage 25*.
In 1927 the picture was presented by the artist
to the Museum of Modern Western Art, Moscow.
In the Hermitage since 1948. Inv. No. 9024

AUGUSTE HERBIN
1882—1960

Auguste Herbin studied painting at the Ecole des Beaux-Arts in Lille. In 1901 he settled in Paris. From 1905 onwards he exhibited at the Salon des Indépendants. In 1910 he took an interest in the first experiments of the Cubists and a year later participated in their exhibitions at the Salon des Indépendants. After 1927 Herbin's painting tended towards the abstract. In 1930 he became a founder member of the Art Concret group which later became known as the Abstraction-Création, and from 1932 to 1936 published an annual of the same name. The artists of this group focused their attention on the problems of a synthesis of painting and architecture, and on industrial design.

Herbin was among the founders of the Salon des Surindépendants.

257   GREEN LANDSCAPE. 1900s
Oil on canvas. 50 × 61 cm
Signed below right: *Herbin*
Provenance: the Auer collection, Petrograd; the State Museum Reserve, Petrograd, 1921; the Museum of the Academy of Arts, Leningrad, 1927.
In the Hermitage since 1945. Inv. No. 10141

258 FLOWERS. *C.* 1907
   Oil on canvas. 81 × 55 cm
   Signed below left: *Herbin*
   Provenance: the Uhde collection, Paris; purchased by
   I. Morozov together with *Portrait* by the same
   author (present whereabouts unknown), 1908; the
   Museum of Modern Western Art, Moscow, 1918.
   In the Hermitage since 1948. Inv. No. 8975

259 MILL ON THE MARNE AT CRÉTEIL
   Oil on canvas. 22 × 33 cm
   Signed below right: *Herbin*
   Provenance: the S. Shchukin collection; the Museum
   of Modern Western Art, Moscow, 1918.
   In the Hermitage since 1948. Inv. No. 9022

ANDRÉ FOUGERON
Born 1913

André Fougeron was born and grew up in Paris. A metal-worker by profession, he could afford painting or drawing only in his spare time. His successful début at the Maison de la Pensée Française (1936), centre of progressive-minded intellectuals in Paris, prompted his decision to devote himself entirely to art. In 1937 and 1938 he displayed his pictures, drawings and water-colours at the Salon des Surindépendants and at the exhibitions "Art cruel" and "Génération nouvelle". He also tried his hand at murals and executed the fresco *Circus* for a students' sanitarium at Saint-Hilaire-du-Touvet (1938). The anti-Fascist orientation of his works (*Tortured Spain*; *Death and Hunger. Spain*) and the vigorous, somewhat rough manner of his painting stamped by Picasso's influence, drew the attention of art critics.

During the Second World War Fougeron was called up and while at the front joined the French Communist Party (1939).

An active member of the French Resistance movement, he let a clandestine printing shop be installed in his studio. He was actively involved in the publication of illegal pamphlets and of the newspapers *Les Lettres Françaises* and *L'Art Français*. Despite the Nazi terror campaign he managed to publish an album of lithographs, *To Win* (1944), and worked on a series of pictures and drawings depicting Paris in the grim days of the occupation (*The Streets of Paris* and others). His participation in the exhibition "Les Etapes du nouvel art contemporain" won him acclaim in the milieu of progressive-minded French intellectuals. In 1942 Fougeron was elected Secretary-General of the National Front of the Arts and in 1946, of the Union of Plastic Arts. He enjoyed the reputation of a leading figure in the new artistic trend of Neo-Realism. In the same year Fougeron received a Prix de peinture for his canvas *Lunch*. His picture *Parisian Women at the Market* (1948) evoked heated arguments and protests on the part of critics because of its almost material representation of a commonplace subject, quite unusual for that time. To the same period belongs his monumental canvas *Hommage à André Houllier* (1949), presented by the artist to the Pushkin Museum of Fine Arts in Moscow.

Fougeron had a number of one-man shows in France, Belgium, the German Democratic Republic, Bulgaria, Hungary, Czechoslovakia, Poland and the Soviet Union. The most important of them all, "The Land of Coalmines" (1951), was devoted to the coalminers of northern France.

Fougeron regularly exhibits at the Salon des Peintres Temoins de Leur Temps. His canvas *Vietnam-67*, displayed there, was awarded a Grand Prix.

In his paintings, drawings, prints, murals, mosaic panels and ceramics the artist eagerly responds to the vital issues of the day, impressing the viewer by a truthful and highly emotional interpretation of the events depicted.

Fougeron is constantly attracted by themes connected with labour and the struggle for peace and democracy; among his more recent subjects is the conquest of space, illustrative of which is a large mosaic panel, *Man of Space* (1962).

260   THE BRIDGE. 1964
Oil on canvas. 195 × 97 cm
Signed below right: *A. Fougeron*
The author's inscription on the back on the canvas:
Le Pont. A. Fougeron
In the Hermitage since 1968 (bought from the artist).
Inv. No. 10046

261 CHAD-FISHERS. 1964
Oil on canvas. 146 × 114 cm
Signed above right: *a. fougeron.*
The author's inscription on the back of the canvas:
Pêcheurs d'aloses. A. Fougeron
In the Hermitage since 1968 (bought from the artist).
Inv. No. 10047

Léon Hubert

Charles Guilloux

Fernand Maglin

Eugène Carrière

Gaston de La Touche

Edmond Barbarroux

Charles Cottet

Georges Dufrenoy

Maurice Lobre

Etienne Moreau-Nélaton

Anatole Hillairet

Lucien Simon

Pierre Lissac

Fernand Piet

Jules Besson

Pierre Girieud

Georges Manzana-Pissarro

Edmond Lempereur

Tony Minartz

Charles Guérin

Charles Hoffbauer

René Seyssaud

Charles Lacoste

Alexandre Troin

Edouard Richard

Charles Picart le Doux

André Favory

Yves Alix

Jean Joveneau

Auguste Chabaud

Louis Charlot

LÉON HUBERT
1887—1915

Léon Hubert was a student of P. de Winter at the Ecole des Beaux-Arts in Lille. He exhibited his works in Lille, Tourcoing and Roubaix. The artist is known mostly for his nocturnal landscapes.

262   SEASHORE IN BRITTANY
Oil on canvas. 46 × 61 cm
Signed below right: *L. Hubert.*
Provenance: acquired by the Museum of Modern Western Art, Moscow, from a private collection, 1937.
In the Hermitage since 1948. Inv. No. 8899

CHARLES GUILLOUX
1866—?

Charles Guilloux, a painter and watercolourist, worked in Paris and from 1892 exhibited at the Salon de la Société Nationale des Beaux-Arts. Landscapes constitute the greater part of his œuvre.

263   MOONLIT NIGHT IN MONTMORENCY.
1897
Oil on canvas. 38 × 62 cm
Signed and dated below right:
C. Guilloux 97
Provenance: the S. Shchukin collection; the Museum of Modern Western Art, Moscow, 1918.
In the Hermitage since 1948.
Inv. No. 8902

FERNAND MAGLIN

Fernand Maglin was active in the late nineteenth and early twentieth centuries. In the 1890s he exhibited at the Salon de la Société des Artistes Français.

264   THE HAMLET. 1898
    Oil on canvas. 41 × 62 cm
    Signed and dated below left:
    F. MAGLIN. 98.
    Provenance: the S. Shchukin collection; the Museum of Modern Western Art, Moscow, 1918.
    In the Hermitage since 1931.
    Inv. No. 6558

265   TOWNSCAPE WITH A CATHEDRAL. 1899
    Oil on canvas. 37.5 × 55 cm
    Signed and dated below right:
    F. Maglin. 99
    Provenance: the S. Shchukin collection; the Museum of Modern Western Art, Moscow, 1918.
    In the Hermitage since 1934.
    Inv. No. 7715

EUGÈNE CARRIÈRE
1849—1906

Eugène Carrière spent his childhood in Strasbourg. From the age of fifteen he mastered the technique of lithography and then copied de La Tour's paintings at Saint-Quentin. In 1870 he was admitted to the Ecole des Beaux-Arts where he attended the class of A. Cabanel. Having graduated from the Ecole he spent a year in London, returned to Paris in 1878 and began to earn his living by making drawings for architectural details and furniture. He made his first successful public appearance in the 1879 Salon, displaying a picture entitled *Young Mother.* Since then on pictures of motherhood and children dominated all his work. Carrière also painted portraits of contemporary writers and artists, the best among them being those of Verlaine, Alphonse Daudet, Anatole France and Rodin. He also did some mural decorations for the Sorbonne and the Hôtel de Ville in Paris.

In the late 1880s Carrière's paintings, with their muted colours and soft silhouettes emerging out of the dimly lit interior, appealed to the Symbolist writers, but in fact his art had nothing to do with Symbolism. In 1890 Puvis de Chavannes and Carrière became founder members of the Société Nationale des Beaux-Arts; in 1898 he established the Carrière Academy. As a teacher he was a man of liberal and independent views, which attracted to his studio the most advanced young artists of his time. Matisse, Derain, Chabaud, Puy and Laprade all studied under him.

266   WOMAN HOLDIND A CHILD
Oil on canvas. 61 × 50 cm
Signed below right: *Eugène Carrière*
Provenance: the P. Shchukin collection; bought by S. Shchukin from his brother, 1912; the Museum of Modern Western Art, Moscow, 1918.
In the Hermitage since 1948.
Inv. No. 9139

267   WOMAN LEANING ON A TABLE
Oil on canvas. 66 × 54 cm
Signed below left: *Eugène Carrière*
Provenance: the S. Shchukin collection; the Museum of Modern Western Art, Moscow, 1918.
In the Hermitage since 1931.
Inv. No. 6565

268   A MOTHER'S KISS
Oil on canvas. 37.5 × 50 cm
Provenance: the I. Ostroukhov collection,
Moscow; the Ostroukhov Museum
of Painting and Icon-painting, Moscow,
1918; the Museum of Modern Western
Art, Moscow, 1929.
In the Hermitage since 1948.
Inv. No. 9140

GASTON DE LA TOUCHE
1854—1913

Gaston de la Touche made his first appearance at the 1874 Salon as a sculptor. In 1879 he began to study engraving under Félix Bracquemond and illustrated Emile Zola's *L'Assommoir*.

The naturalistic manner evident in many of his paintings also betrays the influence of Zola (*The Funeral of a Child*, 1882 Salon; *The Strike*, 1889 Salon, etc.). In the 1890s the artist mainly depicted *scènes galantes* in the Watteau tradition, and took up religious subjects. In 1895, La Touche was among the founder members of the Société des Artistes Français.

269   THE TRANSFERENCE OF HOLY RELICS. 1899
Oil on canvas. 146 × 157 cm
Signed and dated below left:
Gaston de la Touche 99
Provenance: the S. Shchukin collection; the Museum of Modern Western Art, Moscow, 1918.
In the Hermitage since 1948.
Inv. No. 9653

270   THE LAST SUPPER. 1897   ►
Water-colour on paper. 76 × 54 cm
Signed and dated below left:
Gaston la Touche 97
The picture was displayed at the Centenary of French Painting Exhibition in St. Petersburg, 1912 (No. 373).
Provenance: the Z. Ratkova-Rozhnova collection, Moscow; the Tretyakov Gallery, 1917; the Museum of Modern Western Art, Moscow, 1924.
In the Hermitage since 1930.
Inv. No. 42337

EDMOND BARBARROUX
1882—?

Edmond Barbarroux was born and received his artistic education in Toulon. His teachers were Montenard and Cauvin. From 1907 to 1913 Barbarroux constantly took part in the exhibitions of the Salon de la Société Nationale des Beaux-Arts, and from 1913 to 1919 displayed his works at the Salon de la Société des Artistes Français.

He permanently lived in Toulon, painting landscapes of the neighbourhood. In his last years Barbarroux headed the Ecole des Beaux-Arts in Toulon.

271 MOUNTAINOUS LANDSCAPE
Oil on canvas. 50 × 106.5 cm
Signed below left: *E. Barbarroux*
The picture was presented by the artist to the Museum of Modern Western Art, Moscow, in 1935.
In the Hermitage since 1948.
Inv. No. 9103

CHARLES COTTET
1863—1925

Charles Cottet was born at Puy in Haute-Loire into an old Savoy family. In 1882 he settled in Paris and studied painting at the Académie Julian under Maillart and then under Roll. He first exhibited at the Salon of 1889, and sent work to the Gallery of Le Barc de Boutteville. In the 1890s Cottet, Jacques Blanche and René Ménard were among the organizers of the Société Nationale des Beaux-Arts. During these years Cottet worked mostly in Brittany, painting genre scenes and marines. In 1896 he visited Venice and in 1897 exhibited his Venetian landscapes at the Gallery of Art Nouveau. At the 1900 World Exhibition Cottet was awarded a gold medal and in 1911 his one-man show was held. He illustrated the books by André Suarès, *Livre de l'Emeraude* and *La Misère sociale de la femme*.

272 VIEW OF VENICE FROM THE SEA.
1896
Oil on canvas. 55 × 82 cm
Signed below left: *Ch. Cottet*
Provenance: the S. Shchukin collection; the Museum of Modern Western Art, Moscow, 1918.
In the Hermitage since 1948.
Inv. No. 9059

273 MARINE WITH A VIEW OF VENICE.
     1896
     Oil on canvas. 60 × 76 cm
     Signed below right: *Ch. Cottet*
     Provenance: the S. Shchukin collection;
     the Museum of Modern Western Art,
     Moscow, 1918.
     In the Hermitage since 1948.
     Inv. No. 8900

GEORGES DUFRENOY
1870—1942

Georges Dufrenoy received artistic training at the Académie Julian and then in the studio of Laugée. His work reveals a strong influence of Monet. Dufrenoy sent his canvases to the Salon des Indépendants and to the Salon d'Automne. His favourite genres were town views and still lifes.

274   L'HÔTEL DE SOUBISE. 1908
       Oil on canvas. 81 × 100 cm
       Signed below right: *Dufrenoy*
       The picture was exhibited at the Salon d'Automne of 1908 (No. 608).
       Provenance: bought by I. Morozov at the Salon d'Automne, 1908; the Museum of Modern Western Art, Moscow, 1918.
       In the Hermitage since 1931.
       Inv. No. 6571

MAURICE LOBRE
1862—1951

Maurice Lobre studied painting under Gérôme and Carolus-Duran. He painted interiors of the Palace of Versailles, portraits and genre scenes.

275   VESTIBULE OF THE PALACE OF
       VERSAILLES. 1903   ▷
       Oil on canvas. 92.5 × 92 cm
       Signed below left: *M. Lobre. 1903*
       Provenance: the G. Brocard collection, Moscow; the Museum of Fine Arts, Moscow; the Museum of Modern Western Art, Moscow, 1925.
       In the Hermitage since 1948.
       Inv. No. 9061

276   THE DAUPHIN'S ROOM AT THE
       PALACE OF VERSAILLES. 1901   ▷
       Oil on canvas. 80 × 94 cm
       Signed and dated below right:
       M. Lobre 1901
       Provenance: the S. Shchukin collection; the Museum of Modern Western Art, Moscow, 1918.
       In the Hermitage since 1931.
       Inv. No. 6534

ÉTIENNE MOREAU-NÉLATON
1859—1927

Etienne Moreau-Nélaton is known as a painter, graphic artist, one of the most prominent historians of modern art and an important collector of Impressionist works. He was born in Paris and studied under Harpignies. His œuvre includes architectural views, landscapes, interior scenes and portraits. Among the large number of his works on the history of art are monographs devoted to Corot, Fantin-Latour, Edouard Manet, and several catalogues raisonnés devoted to graphics. Moreau-Nélaton bequeathed his art collection to the Louvre.

277   THE PARLOUR. 1900
       Oil on canvas. 60 × 50 cm
       Signed and dated below left: *E. Moreau-Nélaton 1900*
       Provenance: the State Museum Reserve, Petrograd.
       In the Hermitage since 1948.
       Inv. No. 9184

ANATOLE HILLAIRET

Anatole Hillairet worked in the first half of the twentieth century; the information concerning him is scarce. From 1907 he began to exhibit at the Salon des Indépendants. He painted mostly landscapes in the Pointillist technique.

278   LANDSCAPE
Oil on canvas. 52 × 63 cm
Signed below right: *A. Hillairet*
Provenance: the Auer collection, Petrograd; the State Museum Reserve, Petrograd, 1921; the Museum of the Academy of Arts, Leningrad, 1927; the Museum Reserve of the Hermitage, 1931. In the Hermitage since 1948.
Inv. No. 6731

LUCIEN SIMON
1861—1945

Lucien Simon was a pupil of Didier and then of Robert-Fleury at the Académie Julian. From 1885 he exhibited at the Salon de la Société des Artistes Français and from 1893 at the Salon of the Société Nationale des Beaux-Arts. In 1927 he became a member of the Institut de France. His output consists mainly of genre scenes from the life of Breton fishermen. He was also a portrait painter.

279   BRETON MEN AND WOMEN
Oil on canvas. 36 × 47 cm
Signed below right: *L. Simon*
Provenance: the Russian Museum, Leningrad.
In the Hermitage since 1932.
Inv. No. 7442

PIERRE LISSAC
1878—?

Pierre Lissac, painter and cartoonist, was a pupil of Lefebvre and Robert-Fleury. He worked in Paris and from 1900 exhibited at the Salon de la Société des Artistes Français. He also contributed to many illustrated magazines.

280   PROVINCIAL SCENE. 1906
Oil on canvas. 46 × 55 cm
Signed below right: *Lissac*
The picture was exhibited at the Salon d'Automne of 1906 (No. 1056).
Provenance: bought by I. Morozov at the Salon d'Automne, 1906; the Museum of Modern Western Art, Moscow, 1918. In the Hermitage since 1931.
Inv. No. 6567

FERNAND PIET
1869—?

Fernand Piet was a pupil of Cormon, Carrière and Roll. He painted scenes from the daily life of Brittany and exhibited at the Salon de la Société des Artistes Français.

281   THE MARKET IN BREST
Oil on cardboard. 65 × 79.5 cm
Signed below right: *Piet*
Provenance: the S. Shchukin collection; the Museum of Modern Western Art, Moscow, 1918.
In the Hermitage since 1948.
Inv. No. 8989

JULES BESSON
1868—?

Jules Besson, painter and graphic artist, was a pupil of A. Cabanel and Gustave Moreau. From 1894 he sent his works to the Salon de la Société des Artistes Français. He painted scenes from the life of Breton fishermen and miners, and also religious subjects.

282   MINERS
Oil on canvas. 80 × 65 cm
Provenance: the Museum of Modern Western Art, Moscow, 1928.
In the Hermitage since 1948.
Inv. No. 9060

PIERRE GIRIEUD
1875—1940

Pierre Girieud was born and brought up in Marseilles. In 1900 he moved to Paris and there first exhibited at the Salon des Indépendants. In 1902—4 he sent his pictures to Berthe Weil's Gallery, and from 1904 onwards exhibited at the Salon d'Automne. In 1905 Girieud travelled in Italy together with Dufrenoy.

His early works, pre-eminently still lifes with flowers and fruit painted in a highly decorative manner, and his picture *Hommage à Gauguin*, displayed at the Salon d'Automne of 1906, attracted the attention of critics who labelled him a Fauve. These works of Girieud betray the influence of cloisonnisme of the Pont-Aven group.

During his later period the artist devoted himself to monumental murals, painting frescoes and sketches for stained-glass panels. In 1925 he decorated the Metal Tower (Tour de Métaux) at the International Exhibition of Decorative Arts in Paris.

283   PEONIES. 1906
  Oil on canvas. 81 × 65 cm
  Signed and dated above right:
  Girieud. 06
  Provenance: the S. Shchukin collection;
  the Museum of Modern Western Art,
  Moscow, 1918.
  In the Hermitage since 1948.
  Inv. No. 8974

GEORGES MANZANA-PISSARRO
1871—1961

Georges Pissarro, the son of Camille Pissarro, was born in Louveciennes, and spent his childhood in Pontoise and Osny, where he began to study drawing and water-colour under the guidance of his father. At the age of sixteen he went to London and there enrolled in the Arts and Crafts School of William Mor-

ris. He signed his pictures with a double name, Manzana-Pissarro, not to be confused with his father and brothers.

A regular participant in the Salon des Indépendants, Manzana-Pissarro stood for several years at the head of the decorative arts section in the Salon d'Automne. His best-known works include large water-colours on themes from Oriental legends and fairy-tales; he also did book illustrations and painted in oils.

284　ZEBRAS AT A WATERING-PLACE
Gouache and gold on paper. 66 × 53 cm
Signed below right: *G. MANZANA.*
Provenance: the Vollard collection; the I. Morozov collection, 1907; the Museum of Modern Western Art, Moscow, 1918. In the Hermitage since 1931.
Inv. No. 42161

EDMOND LEMPEREUR
1876—1909

Edmond Lempereur worked in Paris and from 1903 exhibited at the Salon des Indépendants.

285   EXPECTATION
(MOULIN DE LA GALETTE). 1905
Oil on canvas. 55 × 46 cm
Signed below left: *E Lempereur*
Provenance: bought by I. Morozov
at the Salon des Indépendants, 1905;
the Museum of Modern Western Art,
Moscow, 1918.
In the Hermitage since 1931.
Inv. No. 6560

286   CORNER OF THE DANCE FLOOR. 1905
Oil on canvas. 46 × 22 cm
Signed below left: *E Lempereur*
Provenance: bought by I. Morozov
at the Salon des Indépendants, 1905;
the Museum of Modern Western Art,
Moscow, 1918.
In the Hermitage since 1948.
Inv. No. 8921

287   THE TABARIN BAR. 1905
Oil on canvas. 61 × 50 cm
Signed below left: *E Lempereur*
Provenance: bought by I. Morozov
at the Salon des Indépendants, 1905;
the Museum of Modern Western Art,
Moscow, 1918.
In the Hermitage since 1948.
Inv. No. 8911

TONY MINARTZ
1873—?

Tony Minartz did not receive any special artistic education. He worked in Paris and exhibited mainly at the Salon des Indépendants, from 1896 to 1914.

288   IN THE THEATRE BOX. 1906
    Oil on canvas. 55 × 46 cm
    Signed below left: *Tony Minartz*
    The picture was exhibited at the Salon des Indépendants in 1906 under the title *Les Spectatrices* (No. 3562).
    Provenance: bought by I. Morozov at the Salon des Indépendants, 1906; the Museum of Modern Western Art, Moscow, 1918.
    In the Hermitage since 1948.
    Inv. No. 8953

289   SORTIE DU MOULIN ROUGE
    Oil on canvas. 55 × 46 cm
    Signed below left: *minartz*
    Provenance: the M. Morozov collection; donated to the Tretyakov Gallery by M. Morozova, 1910; the Museum of Modern Western Art, Moscow, 1925.
    In the Hermitage since 1948.
    Inv. No. 8967

CHARLES GUÉRIN
1875—1939

Charles Guérin was a pupil of Gustave Moreau at the Ecole des Beaux-Arts. He made his first public appearance as a painter at the Salon of the Société Nationale des Beaux-Arts in 1896. He also exhibited at the Salon des Indépendants from 1901 and at the Salon d'Automne from 1903, but mainly sent his works to the Galerie Druet. He illustrated *Fêtes galantes* and *Romances sans paroles* by Verlaine, *Daphnis et Chloé* by Longus and *Manon Lescaut* by l'Abbé Prévost.

During the early years of this century Guérin's showy, brightly coloured canvases appealed to art lovers. His paintings depicting promenades in the parks and *scènes galantes* with the personages dressed in eighteenth century costumes were displayed in many European cities, including Munich (Sezession, 1898, 1900 and 1911), Brussels (La Libre Esthétique exhibition, 1908), Amsterdam (1912), and Rome (the 1913 International Exhibition). After World War One, however, Guérin's works became outmoded and his name ceased to be mentioned either in the press or art literature, although the artist kept on working. In 1923 Guérin was among those who founded the Salon des Tuileries.

290   LADY WITH A ROSE. 1901
Oil on canvas. 52.5 × 37 cm
Signed below left: *Charles Guérin*
Dated on the evidence of the inscription on the back of the canvas: *Charles Guérin 1901*
Provenance: the S. Shchukin collection; the Museum of Modern Western Art, Moscow, 1918.
In the Hermitage since 1934.
Inv. No. 7713

291 YOUNG GIRL WITH A BOOK. 1906
Oil on canvas. 73 × 59.5 cm
Signed below centre: *Charles Guérin*
The picture was displayed in Germany
at the Parisian Artists' Ambulant
Exhibition in 1906.
Provenance: the Druet Gallery; bought
by I. Morozov, 1907; the Museum
of Modern Western Art, Moscow, 1918.
In the Hermitage since 1948.
Inv. No. 9053

292 PROMENADING
Oil on canvas. 79.5 × 168 cm
Signed below right: *ChG*
Provenance: the H. Haasen collection,
Petrograd.
In the Hermitage since 1921.
Inv. No. 4907

293 MUSICIAN. 1907
Oil on canvas. 61 × 47 cm
Signed below right: *Charles Guérin*
Provenance: the G. Brocard collection,
Moscow; the Museum of Fine
Arts, Moscow; the Museum of Modern
Western Art, Moscow, 1924.
In the Hermitage since 1934.
Inv. No. 7712

294   ON THE TERRACE. 1909
    Oil on cardboard. 55 × 46 cm
    Signed below right: *ChG*
    The picture was exhibited at the Salon
    d'Automne of 1909 (No. 698).
    Provenance: the I. Morozov collection,
    1909; the Museum of Modern Western
    Art, Moscow, 1918.
    In the Hermitage since 1948.
    Inv. No. 9067

295   EXPECTATION. 1907
    Oil on canvas. 66 × 55 cm
    Signed above left: *Charles Guérin*
    The picture is dated on the evidence
    of the inscription on the back: *Charles
    Guérin 1907*
    It was exhibited at the Salon of the
    Société Nationale des Beaux-Arts, 1908
    (No. 516).
    Provenance: bought by I. Morozov at
    the Salon, 1908; the Museum of Modern
    Western Art, Moscow, 1918.
    In the Hermitage since 1948.
    Inv. No. 9055

296   SCÈNE GALANTE. 1908
    Oil on cardboard. 45.5 × 54.5 cm
    Signed below right: *Charles Guérin*
    The picture was exhibited at the Salon
    d'Automne of 1908 (No. 861).
    Provenance: the Druet Gallery; the
    I. Morozov collection, 1908; the Museum
    of Modern Western Art, Moscow, 1918.
    In the Hermitage since 1948.
    Inv. No. 9068

297   NUDE. 1907
Oil on canvas. 114 × 88 cm
Signed below right: *ChG*
The picture was exhibited at the Salon
d'Automne of 1907 (No. 729).
Provenance: the Druet Gallery; bought
by I. Morozov at the Salon d'Automne,
1907; the Museum of Modern Western
Art, Moscow, 1918.
In the Hermitage since 1948.
Inv. No. 9115

298   HEAD OF A YOUNG WOMAN. 1909

Oil on canvas. 52 × 50 cm
Signed above left: *ChG*

The picture portrays the model seen
also in the *Nude* (No. 297). It was
exhibited at the Salon d'Automne
of 1909 (No. 699).

Provenance: the Druet Gallery; the
I. Morozov collection, 1913; the Museum
of Modern Western Art, Moscow, 1918.
In the Hermitage since 1934.
Inv. No. 8345

299   PROMENADE IN THE PARK
Oil on canvas. 44 × 54 cm
Signed below left: *Charles Guérin*
Provenance: the M. Morozov collection;
donated to the Tretyakov Gallery by
M. Morozova, 1910; the Museum of Modern
Western Art, Moscow, 1925.
In the Hermitage since 1931.
Inv. No. 6559

CHARLES HOFFBAUER
1875—1915 (?)

Charles Hoffbauer, a pupil of Moreau, Flameng and Cormon, painted pictures on social themes. From 1898 to 1911 he sent his canvases to the Salon de la Société des Artistes Français; among these were *Société bourgeoise du XIVe siècle* (1898), *Le Gueux* (1899) and *La Révolte des Flamands* (1902). For this last picture he received the Rosa Bonheur Prize and a scholarship permitting him to go to Italy. In 1910, together with his friend Bartlett, a sculptor, he went to live in New York. Between 1912 and 1914 Hoffbauer did mural decorations for the Memorial Hall in Richmond, Virginia. During World War One the artist served in the army and did a number of front-line sketches.

300   IN THE RESTAURANT. 1907
Oil on canvas. 114.5 × 166 cm
Signed and dated below right:
Ch. Hoffbauer 07
Provenance: the State Museum Reserve, Petrograd.
In the Hermitage since 1931.
Inv. No. 7319

RENÉ SEYSSAUD

1867—1952

René Seyssaud was born in Marseilles and lived as a child on the family farm at Villes-sur-Auzon. His gifts for drawing and painting developed at an early age. He attended the Ecole des Beaux-Arts in Marseilles, then moved to Avignon where he studied under Grivolas. In 1897 he had his first exhibition at the Gallery of Barc de Boutteville. Soon his works attracted the attention of both art dealers and critics. However, he did not wish to bind himself by contracts. In 1902 Seyssaud settled down at Saint-Chamas in the South of France, where he lived in solitude and was known mainly among local art lovers. He constantly exhibited at the Salon d'Automne, the Salon des Indépendants and the Salon des Tuileries. In 1951 at the Biennale in Menton he was awarded the Grand Prix of the French Provinces.

301   THE ROAD. 1901
    Oil on paper pasted on canvas.
    32 × 49 cm
    Signed below right: *Seyssaud*
    Dated on the evidence of an inscription
    on the back of the canvas: *1901*.
    Provenance: the M. Morozov collection;
    donated to the Tretyakov Gallery
    by M. Morozova, 1910; the Museum
    of Modern Western Art, Moscow, 1925.
    In the Hermitage since 1948.
    Inv. No. 8966

302   PLOUGHLAND
    Oil on cardboard. 45 × 60.5 cm
    Signed below right: *Seyssaud*
    In 1949 the picture was presented
    to the Soviet Union by the citizens
    of Chamas.
    In the Hermitage since 1953.
    Inv. No. 9701

CHARLES LACOSTE
1870—1959

Charles Lacoste was born in Floirac (Gironde). Till 1899 he worked in Bordeaux, then in Paris and in Floirac. Lacoste regularly displayed his works at the Salon des Indépendants (1901—13), the Salon d'Automne (from 1905) and the Salon des Tuileries. He painted landscapes, illustrated books, produced cartoons for tapestries and designed stage settings.

303 HOUSE IN A GARDEN. 1905, August. Mortagne-sur-Gironde
   Oil on cardboard. 25 × 32 cm
   Signed and dated below left: *Charles Lacoste. 1905*
   Signed on the back: *Mortagne-sur-Gironde. Août. 1905*
   Provenance: the S. Shchukin collection; the Museum of Modern Western Art, Moscow, 1918.
   In the Hermitage since 1948.
   Inv. No. 8922

304 SOUTHERN LANDSCAPE. 1912
   Oil on cardboard. 24 × 33 cm
   Signed and dated below left: *Charles Lacoste 1912.*
   The picture was exhibited at the Bernheim-Jeune Gallery in 1914.
   Provenance: purchased by P. Muratov at Lacoste's exhibition in Paris, 1914; bought by the Museum Department of the People's Commissariat for Education, 1920; the Museum of Modern Western Art, Moscow, 1922.
   In the Hermitage since 1948.
   Inv. No. 8942

ALEXANDRE TROIN
1893—?

Alexandre Troin, the son of a vine grower, was born at Favière near Borche (Var). He studied painting on his own, but later also acted on the advice of Cross and Marie Laurencin. The bulk of his works consists of landscapes depicting mainly Provence.

305 LANDSCAPE IN PROVENCE (DEAD FIG-TREE). 1928
Oil on canvas. 50 × 60 cm
Signed and dated below left: *A. Troin 28.*
In 1929 the picture was bought from the artist at Favière by the Museum of Modern Western Art, Moscow.
In the Hermitage since 1948.
Inv. No. 8912

ÉDOUARD RICHARD
1883—?

A pupil of Croisé and Degrave, Edouard Richard exhibited at the Salon des Indépendants, the Salon de la Société Nationale des Beaux-Arts and the Salon de la Société des Artistes Français. Richard became a member of the latter society in 1928.

306   BUNCH OF FLOWERS
Oil on canvas. 43 × 35 cm
Signed below right: *Richard*.
Provenance: the L. Zborowski collection, Paris; donated by L. Zborowski to the Museum of Modern Western Art, Moscow, 1925.
In the Hermitage since 1948.
Inv. No. 8923

307   PLUCKED HEN
Oil on canvas. 27 × 35 cm
Signed below right: *Richard*.
Provenance: the L. Zborowski collection, Paris; donated by L. Zborowski to the Museum of Modern Western Art, Moscow, 1925.
In the Hermitage since 1948.
Inv. No. 8937

CHARLES PICART LE DOUX
1881—1959

Charles Picart le Doux was born in Paris. He studied painting at the Académie Julian and at the Ecole des Beaux-Arts where he enrolled in the studio of Gérôme. In 1904 he first exhibited at the Salon d'Automne, from 1906 sent his works to the Salon des Indépendants and from 1923, to the Salon des Tuileries. Besides oil paintings, mainly landscapes, Picart le Doux did illustrations for books by Baudelaire, Verlaine, Maeterlinck and Colette. He decorated the dining hall of the Lycée in Vincennes and painted the ceilings of the S/S *Normandie*.

308 LANDSCAPE AT SAINT-DENIS
Oil on canvas. 46 × 54 cm
Signed below left: *Picart le Doux.*
Provenance: the Charles Vildrac Gallery; the K. Nekrasov collection, Moscow; the Museum of Modern Western Art, Moscow, 1928.
In the Hermitage since 1948.
Inv. No. 8955

ANDRÉ FAVORY
1889—1937

André Favory was born in Paris. He studied painting at the Académie Julian and from 1919 onwards exhibited at the Salon d'Automne, the Salon des Indépendants and the Salon des Tuileries. During his early period Favory was influenced by Cubism, then showed an admiration for the old masters, especially Rubens. He painted predominantly scenes of leisure amidst nature, and also nudes. In 1927 he was injured in a car accident and during his last years hardly painted at all.

309   FEMALE FIGURE
       Oil on canvas. 72 × 49.5 cm
       Signed below left: *A. FAVORY*
       In 1927 the picture was presented by the artist to the Museum of Modern Western Art, Moscow.
       In the Hermitage since 1948.
       Inv. No. 9123

YVES ALIX
1890—1969

Yves Alix was born in Fontainebleau. From 1908, after graduating from a classical college, he attended the Académie Julian, studying with Dunoyer de Segonzac and Luc-Albert Moreau in the ateliers of Baschet and Royer. Between 1910 and 1912 he was trained under Denis and Serusier at the Académie Ranson where Marquet, Bonnard, Vuillard and Roussel worked at the time.

In 1912 he first exhibited at the Salon des Indépendants and became a member of the Société des Artistes Indépendants. He also sent pictures to the Salon d'Automne and the Salon des Tuileries. During this period he was strongly influenced by Cubism.

On the outbreak of the First World War he signed up as a volunteer. In the 1920s Alix broke with Cubism and turned to the traditions of classical art, particularly of Delacroix and Daumier. Their influence is apparent in Alix's series of paintings and graphic works featuring courtroom scenes, and also in his illustrations for the book *Caractères français*. During his last years Alix gave painting lessons.

310   A SCENE AT COURT. 1928
      Oil on canvas. 61 × 50 cm
      Signed below right: *Yves Alix*
      The picture was painted on the commission of the Museum of Modern Western Art, Moscow, where it was housed since 1929.
      In the Hermitage since 1948.
      Inv. No. 8995

JEAN JOVENEAU
1888—?

Jean Joveneau was born in Paris. He studied painting at the Ecole des Beaux-Arts and then at the Académie Julian under Robert-Fleury. In 1908 he had his first one-man show at the Salon de la Société Nationale des Artistes Français. He also took part in the Sezession exhibition in Rome. He painted portraits, urban landscapes and still lifes.

311 STILL LIFE WITH A MIRROR. 1912
Oil on canvas. 92 × 74 cm
Signed and dated below left:
Jean-Joveneau. 1912
Provenance: the H. Haasen collection, Petrograd.
In the Hermitage since 1921.
Inv. No. 4903

312 STILL LIFE WITH A CAT. 1912
Oil on canvas. 78 × 92 cm
Signed below left: *Jean Joveneau*
Dated on the basis of a comparison with *Still Life with a Mirror* (No. 311).
Provenance: the H. Haasen collection, Petrograd.
In the Hermitage since 1921.
Inv. No. 5109

AUGUSTE CHABAUD
1882—1955

Auguste Chabaud was born in Nîmes. He studied at the local school of fine arts and then attended the Académie Julian and the Académie Carrière where he met Matisse, Derain and Laprade.

In 1901 Chabaud left Paris for Graveson (Provence). There he lived a modest rural life, sometimes sending his works to the exhibitions of the Salon d'Automne (from 1906), the Salon des Indépendants and the Salon des Tuileries.

In 1910 Valentin Serov saw Chabaud's pictures at the Salon d'Automne and was so captivated by his expressive landscapes that he immediately wrote to Ivan Morozov, advising the latter to buy them.

Chabaud also worked as a sculptor, and wrote poetry which he published in several collections: *Poésie pure*, *Peinture pure* and *Le Taureau sacré*.

313   A VILLAGE SQUARE. 1910
Oil on cardboard. 77 × 107.5 cm
Signed below right: *A. CHABAUD.*
The picture was exhibited at the Salon d'Automne in 1910 (No. 10) under the title of *Coin de village*.
Provenance: bought by I. Morozov at the Salon d'Automne, 1910; the Museum of Modern Western Art, Moscow, 1918. In the Hermitage since 1948.
Inv. No. 9086

A. CHABAUD.

LOUIS CHARLOT
1878—1931

Louis Charlot was born at Cussy-en-Morvan (Saône-et-Loire). He studied first under Huet, a tapestry maker from Aubin. In 1898 Charlot settled in Paris. He won the sympathy of Bonnat, who trained him for the entrance competition of the Ecole des Beaux-Arts where the young artist was accepted in the same year.

Charlot first exhibited at the Salon de la Société des Artistes Français in 1901. His landscapes deserved the notice of the critics. He was a member of the Salon d'Automne and displayed his pictures at the Salon des Tuileries. The bulk of his work consists of landscapes of Cussy-en-Morvan where the artist spent the better part of his life.

314   MORVAN VILLAGE BURIED IN SNOW.
      1911
      Oil on canvas. 81 × 100.5 cm
      Signed below right: *Louis Charlot*
      The picture was exhibited at the Salon de la Société Nationale des Beaux-Arts in 1911 (No. 265).
      Provenance: bought by I. Morozov at the Salon, 1911; the Museum of Modern Western Art, Moscow, 1918.
      In the Hermitage since 1948.
      Inv. No. 9174

INDEX

Figures refer to plates

Alix, Yves 310
Barbarroux, Edmond 271
Besson, Jules 282
Bonnard, Pierre 95—105
Boudin, Eugène 8
Carrière, Eugène 266—268
Cézanne, Paul 36—46
Chabaud, Auguste 313
Charlot, Louis 314
Cottet, Charles 272, 273
Cross, Henri 48
Degas, Edgar 30—34
Denis, Maurice 72—92
Derain, André 192—205
Dufrenoy, Georges 274
Dupuis, Georges 130
Fantin-Latour, Henri 1—3
Favory, André 309
Forain, Jean-Louis 35
Fougeron, André 260, 261
Friesz, Othon 177—182
Gauguin, Paul 53—67
Girieud, Pierre 283
Guérin, Charles 290—299
Guillaumin, Armand 21
Guilloux, Charles 263
Herbin, Auguste 257—259
Hillairet, Anatole 278
Hoffbauer, Charles 300
Hubert, Léon 262
Joveneau, Jean 311, 312
Lacoste, Charles 303, 304
Laprade, Pierre 121, 122
La Touche, Gaston de 269, 270
Laurencin, Marie 213, 214
Lebourg, Albert 9
Le Fauconnier, Henri 183—186
Léger, Fernand 254, 255
Lempereur, Edmond 285—287

Lépine, Stanislas 7
Lhote, André 252
Lissac, Pierre 280
Lobre, Maurice 275, 276
Maglin, Fernand 264, 265
Manguin, Henri 126—129
Manzana-Pissarro, Georges 284
Marquet, Albert 131—139
Matisse, Henri 140—176
Minartz, Tony 288, 289
Monet, Claude 10—17
Moreau-Nélaton, Etienne 277
Moret, Henry 68
Ozenfant, Amédée 253
Picart le Doux, Charles 308
Picasso, Pablo 215—251
Piet, Fernand 281
Pissarro, Camille 22, 23
Puvis de Chavannes, Pierre 4, 5
Puy, Jean 123—125
Redon, Odilon 6
Renoir, Auguste 24—29
Richard, Edouard 306, 307
Rouault, Georges 211, 212
Rousseau, Henri 69—71
Roussel, Ker Xavier 93, 94
Seyssaud, René 301, 302
Signac, Paul 47
Simon, Lucien 279
Sisley, Alfred 18—20
Survage, Léopold 256
Troin, Alexandre 305
Vallotton, Félix 108—113
Valtat, Louis 114—120
Van Dongen, Kees 206—210
Van Gogh, Vincent 49—52
Vlaminck, Maurice de 187—191
Vuillard, Edouard 106, 107

FRENCH PAINTING
SECOND HALF OF THE 19TH TO EARLY 20TH CENTURY
THE HERMITAGE MUSEUM

ФРАНЦУЗСКАЯ ЖИВОПИСЬ
ВТОРОЙ ПОЛОВИНЫ XIX — НАЧАЛА XX ВЕКА
ГОСУДАРСТВЕННЫЙ ЭРМИТАЖ

Автор вступительной статьи *Антонина Николаевна Изергина*
Составитель и автор аннотаций *Анна Григорьевна Барская*

Съемка *Л. И. Тарасовой*
Редакторы *А. Н. Слижевская, Н. И. Василевская*
Редактор английского текста *И. Б. Комарова*
Художественный редактор *Г. П. Губанов*
Технические редакторы *Э. В. Малышева,*
Н. К. Соколова
Корректоры *И. Н. Стукалина, В. А. Фатеев*

Издательство „Аврора“, Ленинград, Невский пр., 7/9

Подписано в печать 17/II 1975. Формат 70 × 108¹/₈. Заказ
9083. Изд. № 1178. (29-26). Усл. печ. л. 79,8. Уч.-изд. л. 54,94.

Ордена Трудового Красного Знамени ленинградская типо-
графия № 3 имени Ивана Федорова Союзполиграфпрома
при Государственном комитете Совета Министров СССР
по делам издательств, полиграфии и книжной торговли.
196126, Ленинград, Звенигородская, 11
Футляр отпечатан и изготовлен на ЛФОП 2

Printed in the USSR